Growing Up

Farm Life & Basketball

In the 1940s and '50s

Harold L. Schoen

Printed by CreateSpace, An Amazon.com Company, 4th printing

County Line Publishers, Indianapolis

ISBN-13: 978-1542501859
ISBN-10: 1542501857

Original edition copyright 2015, ISBN-13: 978-1519198631
B &W interior edition copyright 2016, ISBN-13: 978-1533580740

PRAISE FOR *GROWING UP*

"... Schoen grew up in rural western Ohio in a community of German Catholics who, despite having lived in the United States for more than a century, had only recently transitioned to speaking primarily in English....even readers with no connection to that time or place will be charmed by this account. ...." *Kirkus Reviews*

"Reading GROWING UP...was like sitting across the kitchen table with an old friend who might have grown up just down the road, and swapping stories over coffee...Well done. Very highly recommended." *Tim Bazzett,* author of the *Reed City Boy* memoir trilogy

"This is a delightful and honest book...written with such clarity and humility... I'll pass it on to my grandchildren when they want to know how and where grandma grew up." *Madonna Shack*

"...The latter....chapters are filled with [basketball] stories from that era including Red Auerbach scouting an eighth grader named Lew Alcindor (Kareem Abdul-Jabbar), putting the basketball moves on Bill Russell,..." *Donna Seim*, author of *Asante Sana Tanzania.*

"I found it well written, and absorbing on many levels...Hal tells a classic tale of character development from unsure novice, to maybe I'll quit, to maybe I can do this, to conquering hero. What a story. Would make a great movie." *Greg Kohmescher*

"...I loved hearing about the farm work, the Catholic-public school, the emerging sports culture. But more...I had to congratulate Hal and his 12 siblings for rising from humble origins to outstanding accomplished individuals." *Mary Margaret Funk*, author of *Humility Matters: For Practicing the Spiritual Life (The Matters Series)*

DEDICATION

To my sister Ginny

Ginny's diligence and amazing success in school helped me recognize my own potential. Moreover, by resisting some of the limiting attitudes of the older generations, she showed me I could choose to do that too in my own way. Tragically, she died of a brain tumor in 1970, leaving behind her husband and three small children.

CONTENTS

PREFACE

To a large extent, my good friend since high school, Ed Kemper, inspired me to write this memoir. In 2008, Ed was diagnosed with stage-four lung cancer. One doctor told him he may not live more than six months. When Ed passed away on November 16, 2015, he had seen four more grandchildren and a great grandchild. He was an outstanding role model for how to live a full life while fighting a life-threatening disease. He remained active with his family, friends, and church and found time for his volunteer work at a cancer treatment center and his woodworking avocation.

Shortly after his cancer diagnosis, Ed decided to write stories he remembered from his childhood so his descendants have a record. He wrote over 400 pages. How he did all this, I have no idea, but through it all he was his usual very funny self. Seeing Ed writing so productively and with such satisfaction, I was moved to write my own memoirs.

Another motivation came from my siblings after Mom's death in 2012 at age 100. As a group, we began to reminisce more than ever about Mom and Dad and our childhoods, and everyone kept saying someone should write this down. My sister Pat made a great start by putting together a detailed family tree and compiling information from three first-hand sources of memories of our mother, Rose Schoen. It is wonderful for our family to have this record directly from Mom. It gives me hope my descendants will in turn find my memoirs to be of interest.

I think of this memoir as an extended letter to my grandchildren and their descendants to let them know about the long gone world in which I grew to adulthood. More than I expected, reflecting over my life during the writing process has been like therapy for me. As I reflected and wrote, I felt again the idealism, simplicity, enthusiasm, and occasional scares and disappointments of my youth.

My siblings have identified most with the first four chapters because they contain experiences many of us shared. When I got to the high school and college chapters, most of the memories were uniquely my own so of less interest to them. A reader outside my family with an interest in college basketball in the 1950s or 1960s may find the last five, especially the last three, chapters more engaging than the first four. I considered separating these stories but ultimately decided to keep the whole story of my growing up intact as I lived it.

I spent my childhood in the 1940s and 1950s in a west central Ohio farm family of 15 of limited economic means. During those years I saw farming in transition from workhorses and threshing rings to the use of more modern equipment. The farm also served as a huge playground for young children, and I have many fond memories of play on the farm including sports my siblings and I enjoyed – baseball, softball and basketball. The source for another set of remembrances are my elementary and high school experiences, including in sports.

No one in my generation or any previous generations of our family had attended college, but as I grew older and taller circumstances fell into place allowing me to attend the University of Dayton on a provisional basketball scholarship. I was successful in my class work at Dayton, and my basketball memories are of a journey from struggling to make the team, to benchwarmer, to starting forward on the Flyers 1962 National Invitation Tournament (NIT) championship team and senior captain of the team in 1962-63.

My childhood home was a farm located on the Mercer-Darke County Line Road about five miles east of the Indiana state line and six miles from Fort Recovery, Ohio. Darke County, Ohio, is located along the Ohio-Indiana state line. Its county seat,

Greenville, is 40 miles northwest of Dayton and 80 miles north of Cincinnati. Mercer County, also along the state line, is adjacent to Darke County to its north. Fort Recovery, Ohio, where my siblings and I attended high school, is in the southwest corner of Mercer County whose county seat is Celina.

Our farm was 0.5 miles east of point A in Darke County. Sharpsburg is 0.7 miles north of point A.

The present town of Fort Recovery is located at the site of two important Indian battles in the 1790s, the first a devastating defeat for the American soldiers under the command of General Arthur St. Clair. Several years later after a sturdy fort was built on the site of St. Clair's defeat, a few hundred soldiers in the fort led by General Anthony Wayne prevailed against an attack by at least 2,000 Indians. The fort was named Fort Recovery, and a replica of the original fort is a tourist attraction in the town.

The replica fort in Fort Recovery

To write this memoir I referred to the internet for historical information and to Pat's compilation of Mom's memories, but the first six chapters are based mainly on my memories of events. I have tried to be as factually accurate as possible, but I am aware my memory sometimes plays tricks. Something I seem to remember may be gleaned from or distorted by later conversations. My siblings have helped by correcting some of the details I remembered incorrectly, by reminding me of some important events that should be included, and by allowing me to insert some of their memories when they fit well with the narrative. In one or two cases I note one of my siblings disagrees with me about the facts of a childhood incident, and I provide both versions.

I mention many sources of entertainment from the past with little explanation. Rather than try to provide further explanation myself, I invite interested readers to do an internet search on any of the referenced radio shows, comic books, movies, sports figures, or historical events. At present, there is far more information on the internet than anyone will care about concerning these people, products, and events. For example, recordings of many of the radio shows I listened to 65 or 70 years ago can currently be found at http://www.myoldradio.com/old-radio-shows   among   other similar websites.

The chapters that recall my years as a Dayton Flyer are a combination of my impressions and memories and historical information about schedules, scores and individual performances. For the latter, I referred to the internet, newspaper stories from the era, and Ritter Collet's 1989 *The Flyers; A History of University of Dayton Basketball.*

The chart below provides a quick reference to important characters in this memoir.

Paternal Grandparents Jacob Schoen (1874-1965) Elizabeth Knapke Schoen (1877-1965)	*Maternal Grandparents* Bernard Heitkamp (1871-1949) Catherine Gehle Heitkamp (1880-1968)

Parents Arnold Schoen (1904-1986) Rose Heitkamp Schoen (1911-2012) married November 8, 1933	

Children of Arnold and Rose Schoen in birth order	
1. Mary Catherine (Kate) (1934-..)	8. Doris (1947-..)
2. Virginia (Ginny) (1936-1970)	9. Linda (1949-..)
3. Eileen (1937-..)	10. Richard (Rick) (1950-..)
4. Janice (1939-..)	11. Marilyn (1952-..)
5. Harold (Hal) (1941-..)	12. Daniel (Dan) (1954-..)
6. Patricia (Pat) (1943-..)	13. David (Dave) (1955-..)
7. James (Jim) (1945-..)	

1 FAMILY

My parents, Arnold and Rose Schoen (pronounced *Shane*), were both descendants of German Catholic immigrants who spent their lives in or near Mercer County, Ohio. They were in the fourth generation since their ancestors arrived in Mercer County from Germany by way of Baltimore and then Cincinnati in the 1830s and 1840s. The first American generation faced the challenge of establishing a new society in the largely undeveloped western Ohio countryside. They simultaneously cleared much of the land of its dense native forest and gained access to the rich farmland beneath. The nineteenth-century settlers in the southern half of this isolated rural county were predominantly German Catholic immigrants, and the society they developed was based on German customs and language.

In fact, German was the first language of both my parents. For a time their families lived on neighboring farms, and they sometimes socialized and danced together when Mom and Dad were teenagers or younger. In spite of being close neighbors, Mom's family spoke low German, but Dad's spoke high German. Mom said low German was the spoken language of the common people and not a formal written language; in that sense, it had "lower" status than the official high German language. It is

1

more accurate to say there are many dialects of the German language spoken in different parts of Germany. The terms "high" and "low" are geographical references. High German was spoken mainly in the upland and mountain areas of central and southern Germany, and low German was more commonly spoken in the lowlands and flat seacoast in the north. My parents' ancestors migrated to America from different parts of Germany, so the dialects they spoke were not identical.

The German language was used in the local schools in the county until public sentiment against Germany in World War I led to a federal law that forced a change to English. My maternal grandfather, Bernard Heitkamp, could speak little English up to the time of his death in 1949. Into the 21st century, Mom and her siblings spoke German to each other when they visited. Dad's family members all spoke some German but they had moved more toward the use of English than the Heitkamps. I had a marvelous opportunity to learn German as a child, but neither my parents nor I valued having me learn a second language at the time.

The most common reaction to the German language for my siblings and me was to mimic some German pronunciations that sounded funny to us, such as, pronouncing "w" as "v" and "in" as "een". In spite of our making fun, the German language had a significant influence on our English speech patterns. For example, we had a recent family party at a restaurant in St. Wendelin, which we all still pronounced "Wenleen" or "Venaleen." German also includes frequent use of the sound "ack" or "ach," as when Mom often cautioned, "Ach! If you kids don't stop that, somebody is going to end up crying." Although we sometimes ignored Mom's usually on-target warning, my brother Jim and I were so impressed with that sound we often begin our written communications with "Ach! Ach! Ach!"

As was typical in the farm culture of their childhoods, both Arnold and Rose attended one-room country elementary schools and, although both were good students, neither completed high school. From about age ten, Arnold stopped attending school each year in March so he could help on his father's farm. After eighth grade, with his parents' approval, he dropped out of school entirely.

Rose quit school at 16 years of age. She said she had only completed grade nine though her teachers urged her parents to allow her to complete high school. She then began to work as a "hired girl" for families in the area who needed and could afford extra live-in help with housework and childcare. Until Arnold and Rose were over sixty and they went to visit some of their children who had left the area, neither had been much more than a hundred miles from home.

Married in the midst of the great depression, Rose Mary Heitkamp and Arnold Peter Schoen, who were never accustomed to luxury, had a difficult start financially. This tough beginning set the tone for their future. They never earned more than $4,000 in a year as they were raising their thirteen children. Immediately following their wedding, Arnold and Rose moved onto a farm owned by Jacob (Jake) Schoen, Arnold's father where they were to reside for the next

Arnold and Rose, November 8, 1933

33 years. Fortunately, working the farm provided a steady source of food for the family.

The farm originally consisted of 137 acres. It was located along the Mercer-Darke County Line Road on the Darke County or south side. Although the farm was inside the border of Darke

3

County, the children went to school and the adults did most of their business in Mercer County. The farm was six miles from Fort Recovery (1950 population – 828) and one and one-half miles from Sharpsburg. Sharpsburg did not have the 50 residents required by the state of Ohio for incorporation as a town so it was officially referred to as a "crossroad population center".

Within a year of their marriage, Rose gave birth to her first child, Mary Catherine. Twelve others followed at a regular rate of about one every two years for the next 25 years. Almost miraculously, all were born healthy and free of physical or mental disabilities. At least one son or daughter and as many as thirteen lived in my parents' home for more than forty years of their married lives.

I was born on May 7, 1941, exactly seven months before Japan's surprise attack on Pearl Harbor that provided the impetus for America's entry into World War II. I was the fifth child and the first son. At my birth, Janice was two years old, Eileen was four, Ginny was five, and Kate was seven. Before I was two, another sister, Pat, was born, and when I was not yet four my first brother, Jim, came along. He would become my closest childhood companion. The next ten years brought six more siblings—Doris, Linda, Rick, Marilyn, Dan, and Dave, in that order.

Everyone in the family referred to our mother as "Mom" and our father as "Daddy". In our presence, our parents referred to each other in this way as well, rarely using the other's first name. In conversations about Daddy after his death in 1986 at age 82, that childish sounding name was natural for Mom and most of my adult siblings. As an adult I began to refer to him as "Dad," although sometimes in the company of brothers and sisters I still revert to "Daddy."

My Grandma Schoen, a midwife, assisted Mom in my delivery at home. On my sixtieth birthday, Mom told a story about my birth that gives a window into her life of duty, work and constancy. According to Mom, "It was a muddy day. I had to keep mopping, because Daddy and the kids kept tracking in. I knew I was in labor, so I worked on dinner, the noon meal, because Grandma needed to eat. It worked out well. Harold was born, and she had dinner afterwards. Later that week Daddy took the baby down to church in Sharpsburg to be baptized." Grandma Heitkamp came and stayed with the family for a week or two while Mom recuperated from the birth.

* * *

As for some of my earliest memories, I vaguely remember Jim's birth and being excited about having another boy in the family. I also remember listening to Mom, Dad, and other adults talking during or right after World War II about rationing of groceries, Harry Truman becoming president when Franklin Roosevelt died, Truman's decision to drop the horrific, newly invented atomic bomb on Japan, auto companies not manufacturing any new model cars during the war, and worries about Mom's youngest brother Melvin who was serving in the army in Europe.

My sister Janice, two years older than me, remembers Mom taking the two of us with her in the car to the canning factory in St. Henry. While she went inside briefly, we were in the car when two German prisoners of war who were interred in Mercer County and working at the canning factory came by. Janice and I shyly hid down in the back seat, but they laughed and talked to us in German. They wanted to know my name and when we said "Harold" they pronounced it with a heavy German accent we later laughed about. I remember as a four-year-old the celebrations of the surrender of Germany (VE day) and of Japan (VJ day), or at least I remember the happy talk of the adults as they participated in or recalled those two glorious days.

When I was very young, the rare appearance of an airplane in

5

the sky prompted a yell to others in the family not to miss the sight. Occasionally, a hobo came walking down our then gravel road and stopped for food. Mom and Dad always greeted these complete strangers warmly, talked to them with great interest about their plight, and fed them a meal. They did not blame the hobos for being destitute, but rather attributed their situation to bad luck and the devastating effects of the great depression.

By necessity, our family life was dominated by practicality and frugality. Dad was what was called a general farmer. At any particular time, he owned seven to twelve milk cows, about a hundred hogs, several hundred laying hens, and, until the late 1940s, two workhorses. Annually he raised 15 to 20 acres each of corn, oats, winter wheat, hay, and soybeans. In a truck garden and orchard, Dad and Mom had several types of vegetables, Concord grapes, sorghum, popcorn, and apples entirely for family use.

Each spring we went to the chicken hatchery in Sharpsburg and got several hundred baby chicks of mixed gender. We fed them for a few months in our brooder shed. When they were big enough, we put the hens into the henhouse or "chicken coop" and began to butcher the roosters, seven to ten at a time, to eat for Sunday dinners until the supply was gone.

These delicious "spring chicken" dinners with mashed potatoes, gravy, and two or three fresh vegetables from the garden hold a special place in my memory. We loved this food so much we sat impatiently through grace before the meal with our forks at the ready and, at "Amen," raced our siblings to the mashed potatoes or chicken. Neil Diller, Pat's husband, jokes that the reason seven of 13 of us are left-handed is we made the sign of the cross with our right hand and grabbed for food with our left.

* * *

Dad was mainly responsible for feeding and caring for the animals and planting and harvesting the crops, but at busy times this was too much work for one person. Mom and the kids helped Dad with the outside work as needed. Before I was old enough to be of much help, Mom and my older sisters often helped in the fields, and they each hand-milked a couple of cows every morning and evening. My brothers and I took over more of that work as we got older, but except for my youngest sister Marilyn all the girls learned to milk so they could be called into duty if needed.

Dad did not take an active part in raising the children. This is not a comment on him so much as on the rural culture of that generation. The women raised the kids; the men did the outside work in the barn and the fields. While the women were expected to help with outside work if needed, the men were *never* expected to help with work in the house. For example, I never washed a dish or a piece of clothing while living in my parents'

Mom, Pat, Jim, Doris, and Linda

home. My sisters shined everyone's Sunday shoes, including mine.

Mom seemed well-adjusted to a life of hard work as a farm wife and mother. While she was shy and quiet in social groups, with children and weather being her main topics of conversation, as a mother she usually gave us support when we needed it. Her relatively undemanding personality allowed us freedom to develop our own interests within the limitations of our environment, and her dependability and steadiness gave us feelings of security.

Not all of my brothers and sisters felt as favorably toward Mom as I. She was stricter and more controlling of my older sisters than of the boys or the younger girls. For example, Mom insisted my older sisters wear slacks in high school gym class rather than shorts like most of the other girls, a source of embarrassment for them. As teenagers, they had stricter time deadlines for getting home when they went out at night than my younger sisters, and my brothers and I had no time limits other than our coach's training rules when we were in a sports season. Perhaps the daily effort and stress involved in raising such a large number of children led Mom to gradually loosen her rules and restrictions.

The externals of life for me as a child were plain and uncomfortable by most standards. We lived in a big drafty old farmhouse that was hot in the summer and cold in the winter. The first floor consisted of a kitchen, dining room, living room which for a number of years was used as a bedroom in the winter, and my parents' bedroom—all large rooms with high ceilings. Also on the first floor were two big pantries, one for laundry and the other for storing wood and coal in the winter. We referred to the latter as "the slop bucket pantry" because it harbored a five-gallon bucket for garbage. The garbage was fed to the hogs each day.

The second floor of the farmhouse contained three bedrooms. In my high school years when all thirteen children were living at home, four of us slept in each upstairs bedroom in the summer. During the winter, some of the younger kids moved downstairs and slept in the somewhat warmer living room or "front room". The baby in the family at the time slept in a baby bed in Mom and Dad's bedroom.

Until near the end of World War II, we had no electricity on the farm; there were no power lines available on our rural road. Before electricity, we used kerosene lamps for lighting in the house. For evening entertainment in addition to board games and cards, we had a big, battery-powered radio we all sat around as closely as needed to hear the crackly transmission of radio dramas and comedies. As Mom carried a lamp to help us to our beds at night, the deep, dark, flickering shadows were like those I imagined as I listened to scary radio shows like *Inner Sanctum* and its ominous creaking door. Another, *The Shadow*, began each episode with an eerie-voiced, "Who knows what evil lurks in the heart of man? The Shadow knows," followed by maniacal laughter.

I remember the exciting day the electric company men installed our transformer, and Dad's older brother Roman (Bones), who was handy with electrical wiring, helped to wire the house. After we had electricity, Mom and Dad bought a used "Frigidaire," as they called any refrigerator, to replace the icebox we kept in the cellar. The radio, now electrically powered, continued to be an important source of entertainment for us. We had no telephone while I lived at home, and I was in high school when we got our first black-and-white television set in 1957.

With no telephone to communicate about visiting, Mom or my sisters baked a cake or some cookies every Saturday or Sunday so they had a special treat available in case the families of neighbors or uncles and aunts dropped in for a visit on Saturday or Sunday. At the end of these visits, the guests usually said, "Now it's your turn to come to our house," so for each family in our social network we had an approximate idea of when to expect a visit from them and when to plan a visit to their house.

In the winter, our house was heated by a wood- and coal-burning stove located in the dining room. The stove was sufficiently powerful to heat the dining room and kitchen, although it could not keep out all the cold drafts. Some heat was left for the downstairs bedroom and front room after my parents opened the doors to those rooms when they went to bed. The fire was allowed to go out during the night, and Dad re-started it around 5:30 each morning. A vent located directly above the stove allowed some heat to reach the upstairs east bedroom and, by keeping upstairs doors open, a little heat got to the north bedroom. The barely insulated upstairs west bedroom, furthest from the stove and battered by the northwesterly winter wind, was so cold we didn't use it in the winter keeping its door closed.

The thermometer in the boys' room, the north bedroom upstairs, sometimes read less than 25 degrees Fahrenheit on cold winter mornings. When it snowed during the night, we routinely wiped a thin layer of snow off our bed covers where it settled as it sifted in around the windowpanes. On mornings like those I jumped hurriedly out of bed, usually around 6:30, grabbed my clothes, and with the support of the stair rail vaulted down several steps at a time in my hurry to get downstairs where I stood near the stove for warmth.

Indoor running water was a luxury we lacked until the mid-fifties, and then it was only cold drinking water from an outdoor-style faucet Dad installed near the kitchen sink. For drinking water in the house before that, Dad, with the help of us kids as we became old enough, carried buckets of water to the house that we had hand-pumped from the deep well in the barnyard. The porcelain water bucket was placed on the counter in the kitchen, and we drank from it using a long-handled dipper.

Rainwater from the house roof and downspouts was caught in the cistern located in the yard near a corner of the house formed by the kitchen and pantry. Using a hand pump mounted at the end of the kitchen sink, we pumped this soft water from the cistern to use for laundry and cleaning. Jim has an unpleasant memory of Dad lowering him into the cistern to clean it; he was little enough to fit easily through the opening at the top.

Indoor bathrooms in the 1940s were a rarity on Mercer County farms. While much more common in the 1960s, they never made an appearance in the Arnold Schoen farmhouse. It was in 1967 when my parents moved off the farm that they first lived in a house with a bathroom. On the farm, we had a smelly "two-holer" outhouse or toilet in the barnyard. At night, we shared two chamber pots, one downstairs in Mom and Dad's bedroom and one upstairs. These were lidded metal buckets holding about two gallons for use if we felt the urination urge during the night. Mom or one of my older sisters emptied the pots into the outdoor toilet each morning. As we got old enough, we kids were expected to help with nearly every task on the farm, but I will forever be grateful to Dad that we never had to shovel out the outhouse. He always did that extremely unpleasant job himself.

Outhouse juts off tractor shed, and chicken coop is to the left. Hog house is in background. It must be a Monday, since the laundry is hanging out to dry.

For our weekly baths on Saturday nights, we heated kettles of rainwater on the kitchen stove, poured them into a washtub, moderated the temperature with cold water, added soap, and took our bath in the kitchen. The washtub was large enough for littler kids to sit in, but as we got older we stood beside the tub and washed our bodies with a washcloth dipped into the soapy liquid in the tub. It was not practical to change the water in the tub for each of us, so we were often washing with water already used by one or two others. For a little privacy, we shut the doors and pulled the curtains in the kitchen.

Not surprisingly, none of us liked these bathing conditions, and we took advantage of alternatives whenever we could. A few years ago when Jim was inducted into the Fort Recovery High School Athletic Hall of Fame he joked, "The main reason we played sports in high school was so we could take showers in the locker room."

When summer temperatures reached the 90s and lower 100s, our house was sweltering until 11:00 pm or later. To escape the indoor heat, on many of those hot summer evenings Mom and Dad sat on the kitchen porch; Mom in the swing usually with at least one of the littler kids beside her or on her lap and Dad in his wooden rocking chair with the radio tuned to a Cincinnati Reds baseball game. Meanwhile, the older kids played games like hide and seek, andy-over, and a version of tag we called Old Gray Wolf, running all around the house yard and at times into the barnyard. The security and joy I felt on those summer evenings, laughing and playing with my brothers and sisters while Mom and Dad relaxed nearby, are among my fondest childhood memories.

Our house had two porches; a cement porch off the kitchen my parents often used on summer evenings and a wooden porch on the northwest side of the house off the front room. Mom and Dad did not use the wooden front porch, but we kids often played there. A neat activity I remember on that porch was an idea of my older sisters. I was ten or eleven when they decided to plan and put on plays on the front porch using all of the kids who were old enough in the cast. Janice was usually the author of these plays. We practiced the play a few times, then in the evenings after milking or on the weekend Mom and Dad brought chairs around to watch the play from the yard in front of the porch. In one, an actor, Linda or Marilyn, had a death scene. In the process of dying the actor accidentally fell off the stage into a flowerbed next to the porch to hearty laughter from the audience and her fellow actors.

Our house in the mid-sixties with Jim and two younger siblings; wooden porch is to the right.

* * *

In his retirement, Grandpa Schoen helped Dad on the farm most summer days until aches and pains of old age caused him to discontinue the practice in the early 1950s. Dad and Mom were buying the farm from Grandpa, and he had strong opinions about how it should be operated. Grandpa was an assertive, forceful person compared to Dad, who, while he had a quick but controlled temper when we kids annoyed him, was a pleasant, quiet man who was well-liked in the community. Mom felt Dad allowed Grandpa, who had old-fashioned ideas about farming, to push him into unwise farming practices.

For example, one year Grandpa decided he and Dad could save money by building their own corn picker using parts from junkyards in the area. Over Mom's objections, they pursued the idea with limited success. After struggling for over a year to find parts compatible enough to mesh in one machine, Dad and Grandpa assembled a picker that worked briefly at the start of the corn harvest before breaking down. After a delay of a day or two to fix the problem, the picker again worked only briefly before another breakdown. After two or three such frustrating breakdowns, they began to worry the yield would be hurt if the corn were left in the field any longer. With some embarrassment, they borrowed my Uncle Lee's picker to pick the remainder of our corn.

My Grandma (Elizabeth) and Grandpa (Jacob) Schoen in 1951.

Being the oldest boy, I was a favorite of my Grandpa Schoen who called me "Big Un." One of my early vivid memories is of a day when Dad and Grandpa were planning to drive to Winchester, Indiana about thirty miles away to get a part from a junkyard for the corn picker. I was about five years old and wanted to go along. Going along to "town" was a great treat in my childhood, even if "town" was only Sharpsburg, which it usually was. So, at age five, Winchester (1950 population – 5,467) sounded better to me than a trip to Paris may sound to a middle-class child today.

As a punishment for some misbehavior earlier that day, Mom decided I couldn't go. In retaliation, I threw a major kicking and screaming tantrum during which Mom's anger grew to the boiling point. Eventually, I regained my composure and went out to the barnyard where Dad and Grandpa were just preparing to leave. Grandpa waved and said, "Want to come along, Big Un?" I was in the car before Mom knew what was happening. I don't recall anything about the trip or what happened afterward, but the incident probably aggravated the sore point between Mom and Dad concerning Grandpa's role on the farm.

I was a tall, skinny child with light blond hair. In my pre-school years I was more interested in helping Mom sew and iron than in typical boys' activities, an interest Grandpa Schoen did his best to discourage. He had me tag along with him in the summertime. I remember being glad for his attention, but I also was sensitive to the tension between Grandpa and Mom. Against Mom's better judgment one day, Grandpa let Jim and me ride on the back of the old Farmall tractor while he cultivated a field. In a particularly rough spot of ground one of us was thrown off and cut slightly by the disk before Grandpa could stop. Jim remembers he fell off the tractor, and he may be right but I am not sure. At any rate, this incident ended our riding on the back of the tractor in the field.

Another area of disagreement between Grandpa and Mom was the condition in which the men kept the barnyard. Most of it was a mess; long unkempt grass and piles of useless wood and metal parts from machinery strewn irregularly in it. Mom complained occasionally to Dad but he didn't care about the issue

Ginny worked to keep the yard neat.

enough to get involved. Grandpa was the stumbling block to cleaning up the barnyard. When my sister Ginny was in high school, she decided to take charge. Ginny liked order and neatness, so she had little patience with Grandpa's argument that keeping the barnyard cleaned up was a waste of time and energy that could be better spent on more productive work.

One day she just decided to clean up the messy barnyard. She got the help of several of her siblings including me. We loaded our trailer with the scrap iron and other junk and took it to the junkyard near Fort Recovery. We cut the longer grass first with the tractor and hay mower and then with a lawn mower. After the first cutting the grass was stubbly and brown, but when it grew and was mowed again its appearance improved a lot. Grandpa said we were wasting our time, but he gave up when the barnyard looked much better than it had before. We were also able to play softball and other games on parts of it that had been covered with junk-strewn long weeds and grass.

* * *

In our rural culture, we were treated differently from the children of affluent professional parents today. Two popular adages for parents at the time were, "Children are to be seen and not heard" and "Spare the rod and spoil the child." In social gatherings of adults and children, the children were expected to be quiet and not interfere with the adults' conversation unless they were addressed specifically. The adults, who wanted to socialize without interruption, soon told the children to "go out and play," knowing the farms we lived on provided marvelous outdoor playgrounds. Even on rainy days, the barn was an inviting environment for imaginative play, so we did not feel offended to be sent outside; on the contrary, we were happy when it happened.

Up to about ten years of age, if we misbehaved beyond a certain point, our parents spanked us, sometimes with a belt or switch. Mom and Dad did not spank us often and usually not with much anger or severity, but they believed it was their duty to do so in some instances and we would be better people as a result. Their belief about spanking was reinforced by their contemporary society and by the Catholic Church.

Our family was usually in survival mode economically. We never ate at restaurants or took vacation trips and we didn't expect or receive many material things. A few toys at Christmas, some candy at Christmas, Easter, and St. Nicholas Day (December 6), a dollar on our birthdays, and one or two changes of clothes for school were standard fare. Praise from our parents was also in short supply. When one of their children did well in school or in a sport, Mom and Dad were obviously proud, but they tempered their reaction advising not to forget "you are no better than anyone else" and "don't go getting a big head."

I was painfully shy around adults. Living in the semi-isolation of the farm, the vast majority of my social contacts were members of my immediate family. When other adults, usually aunts, uncles, or neighbors, made infrequent visits I hid behind Mom or Dad. If an adult spoke to me I was embarrassed and rarely had the nerve to answer. For a few years, I hid from the milkman in the morning if I was not finished with morning milking when he came to pick up our milk. As I got older, I was able to control this behavior, but the natural tendency toward shyness was always part of my introverted adult personality. My first reaction to a social invitation is usually negative, sometimes even dread, but if I decide to participate I often have a pleasant time.

As a child in such a huge family, I drew emotional strength from being part of a large and stable group but I rarely felt important as an individual. Mom's attention had human limits and was directed mainly toward the two youngest children at any given time. By about age four I had to compete for parental love and attention with my sisters, a competition in which winning was little consolation. It only subjected me to more teasing from them, which led me to deny their accusations of favoritism even though they were sometimes right. As an adult, I came to appreciate that the feeling of security I gained from being in a family with steady and dependable parents outweighed a few painful moments brought on by sibling rivalry. I also realized regretfully late in life that, as the oldest boy, I dished out plenty of teasing that was sometimes hurtful to my siblings.

Overt signs of affection in our family were rare, but the constancy of our parents and their obvious commitment to our care even when life was difficult for them assured us we were safe and secure. My siblings and I do not often express affection to one another even now, although some of us have recently begun to hug each other when saying hello and goodbye. In any case, the life experiences we have shared and continue to share with the common joys and sorrows have cemented bonds of familial love.

* * *

The farm provided our family with much of our food but for some groceries and supplies we needed an outside source. When I was young, traveling salesmen and "hucksters" came by our farm to sell items we may need. Jim reminded me that we continued until the mid-fifties to have visits from Edmund Bertke, who sold a wide variety of McNess products including coconut oil shampoo that Mom usually bought. Fuller Brushes were also a popular item for home salesmen, made more popular by the 1948 movie *The Fuller Brush Man*, a comedy starring Red Skelton.

Another merchant who came regularly to our farm was the Buck's Corner huckster. Buck's Corner was a rural crossroad with a small grocery store located about nine or ten miles southwest of our farm. The storeowner renovated a school bus, removing the seats and installing shelves on either side of the aisle. He stocked the bus with a selection of his groceries and cleaning products he thought local farm families would be interested in buying. He then made the rounds of the nearby farms, pulling into barnyards and displaying his wares. I think he came by our farm once or twice a month, and my parents bought an item from him if they had an immediate need for it. But his prices were higher than at stores in Sharpsburg and other surrounding towns, and he went out of business about the time I entered elementary school.

In my pre-school years, it was a big deal to make the trip to Sharpsburg. Formerly called Zenz City, Sharpsburg consisted of an elementary school, St. Paul's Catholic Church and rectory, Forthofer's Grocery, the Farm Bureau Feed Mill, Klingshirn's chicken hatchery, and perhaps six or eight private homes. Dad made bi-monthly trips to the Sharpsburg Feed Mill with a trailer filled with sacks of oats and corn to be ground for cattle, chicken, and hog feed. Forthofer's grocery store/saloon provided Mom with groceries and Dad with an occasional opportunity for a beer and a talk with his neighbors. Mom and Dad and all the kids over seven years old attended one of the two masses each Sunday morning at St. Paul's Catholic Church.

Grandpa and Grandma Schoen lived in one of the Sharpsburg houses, their retirement home. In 1967, Mom and Dad retired to the same house. Grandpa had a blacksmith shop across the driveway from their house where he spent a great deal of time when he was not helping on our farm. Directly across the road from our grandparents' house was the late 19th century Victorian-style Zenz house. It wasn't fancy or large, perhaps 2,500 square feet on two floors with an unfinished basement, but its interesting architectural style distinguished it from the area's mid-western farmhouses that were mainly shaped like rectangular boxes partitioned into smaller rectangular rooms. To the younger Schoen kids, the Zenz house was a castle.

Sometime in the mid-1950s Bill and Olivia (Dad's oldest sister "Leefa") Miller and family bought the Zenz house and lived there for perhaps ten years. It was clear during family visits

The Zenz House

with the Millers the house had not been well maintained. It was cold and drafty in the winter and hot in the summer, not the comfortable castle we had fantasized. After hosting a few other resident families, the Zenz House was torn down in the 1980s and replaced by an office for the feed mill next door. This was an understandable decision by the owner, but to me it was the loss of Sharpsburg's most unusual attraction.

On nearly every trip to Sharpsburg, we dropped in for a brief visit with Grandpa and Grandma Schoen. Grandma Schoen was a social person who enjoyed having us stop by. Jim reminded me she was an avid fan of professional wrestling on television. She despised the "villain" wrestlers, Magnificent Maurice and Handsome Johnny Baron. Another target of her contempt was a female heckler named Bouncing Beulah. Those visits and Grandpa Schoen's regular presence on our farm in the summer meant we saw a great deal of our paternal grandparents until they died in 1965 within a few days of one another.

We saw much less of Grandma and Grandpa Heitkamp. Grandpa was bedridden in their home in St. Henry during the years I remember him, and he died of cancer on Christmas night, 1949.

That Christmas day, Dad's siblings and their families were invited to Grandma and Grandpa Schoen's house for the afternoon and evening. Everyone knew Grandpa Heitkamp was near death, so Mom and Dad were at first unsure what our family should do. They decided Mom would go to her parents' house where her brothers and sisters were assembled to be with Grandma and Grandpa Heitkamp, and I think one or two of my older sisters went with her. Dad and the rest of the kids went to his parents' house to celebrate Christmas and play with our cousins on the Schoen side of the family.

Grandma and Grandpa Heitkamp at Eileen's First Communion, May 1944. Our cement porch is behind.

That night, soon after supper, Mom's brother Al came by to report their father had died. It was touching for me to see Dad's family also grieved the loss of Grandpa Heitkamp. They reminisced about the fun they had as teenagers living on neighboring farms when Grandpa Heitkamp played the accordion and Grandma Heitkamp played the harmonica. They remembered moving the kitchen and dining room furniture aside and dancing to Grandpa and Grandma's music. To add to their fun, Mom's brother Bennie was a caller for square dances, a form of dancing that is popular in the area to this day.

Grandpa Heitkamp was the first family member whose death I remember. The hardest part for me was to see Mom's deep grief. Although I don't remember much about Grandpa

Heitkamp, Mom said he was a kind and gentle man, honest and hardworking. Mom grew up on a farm near Maria Stein in southeastern Mercer County, but in 1931, early in the great depression, the bank foreclosed on her father's farm, and her parents began to depend on their children's jobs to help with the family's living expenses. According to Mom, this turn of events was difficult for Grandpa Heitkamp whose health soon began a steady decline.

Another sorrow for Mom's family was that two of her brothers had serious life-long problems with alcohol. Mom said they began to drink during the period when alcohol was prohibited by constitutional amendment. Were it not for prohibition, she thought they would not have had these problems.

Grandma Heitkamp, a quiet, shy person, outlived her husband by nearly 20 years. After Grandpa died, she lived alone for a while in St. Wendelin, a crossroad population center even smaller than Sharpsburg. Knowing Grandma was lonesome, Mom thought it would be nice if I rode my bike the three or four miles to visit her. I'm not sure why Mom wanted me rather than one of her other children to make the visit, but I resisted at first due mainly to shyness. In the end, Mom wore down my defenses, and I rode my bike to see Grandma Heitkamp one summer afternoon. It turned out to be a pleasant visit. We played cards and ate watermelon, two of my favorite activities then and now. I don't remember other details of the visit, but I'm sure we didn't talk much.

For supplies and services not available in Sharpsburg, my parents relied on other towns in the area. Our barber and auto mechanic were in Burkettsville, three miles east of our farm with a 1950 population of 211. Our dentist's office was about eight miles away in St. Henry (1950 population – 715), but we depended mainly on Fort Recovery for our doctor, shoe shop, furniture store, clothiers, hardware, drug store, five-and-dime stores, and banks. When Dad or Mom needed these services or supplies, one of them drove the six miles northwest to Fort Recovery, usually taking some of their kids along. We eagerly anticipated those trips. It was most fun to go with Dad who usually stopped at Sauer's Drug Store & Soda Fountain for a soda or malt.

A great entertainment for us kids when I was in elementary school was the Fort Recovery Harvest Jubilee. Each July, the town merchants sponsored this weeklong street carnival with exciting rides, great food, and tent stands that offered "swell" prizes if you succeeded at their games of skill. Professional acrobats and balloonists were hired to perform daily shows; each day during the Jubilee we could see the 4:00 pm balloon ascension from our farm.

Through the 1940s and early 1950s, Mom usually shopped for clothes and for Christmas toys in Fort Recovery or by mail from *Sears & Roebuck, Spiegel's* and *Alden's* catalogues. In later years, she or one of my older sisters took us shopping once or twice a year, usually in August before school started and again before Christmas, in one of the four nearby larger towns – Portland (Indiana), Coldwater, Celina or Greenville (1950 populations – 7,064, 2,217, 5,700 and 8,859, respectively). Those shopping trips were the only opportunity I had, as a kid, to see how "urban" living differed from my farm experience.

From a young age, my siblings and I were expected to help with various chores on the farm, and those chores were a big part of our lives.

2 WORK

To me, the farm was a safe island designed just for our family. It provided our food and was the site of most of our daily activities. We left to go to school and church, run errands and so on, but we always returned to the safety of our island. The farm was a workplace and a playground for the expanding family of growing Schoen kids. There was always work for us to do, but with our large group of siblings we were never without companions to share in the tasks.

In the summers when we were in elementary school, we went with Mom or older siblings to pick raspberries, blackberries, and elder berries in nearby woods. Mom made jelly or jam from the berries that were left after we had our fill as we picked them. The house and garden required lots of work including childcare, cooking, laundry, ironing, housecleaning, gardening, canning, and sewing, but this was the realm of Mom and my sisters.

My older sisters had a lot of child care duties. Kate, the oldest, remembers her job when Jim was born. Jim was the first of Mom's children born in the hospital so she was concerned about her absence from home and about getting to the hospital in time for the birth. She woke ten-year-old Kate at 4:00 a.m. on February 7, 1945, Jim's birthday, to give her orders for the day.

Kate was to stay home from school, but eight-year-old Ginny and seven-year-old Eileen were to go on the bus. Ginny wouldn't do what Kate said, so Mom couldn't have them work together. It was also Monday and therefore washday. Mom had been up all night doing the laundry. The clothes had been washed and were waiting in the rinse tubs. Kate was to put the clothes through the wringer and hang them on the clothesline while she also cared for six-year-old Janice, me at less than four years old, and two-year-old Pat until Daddy got home from the hospital.

* * *

Indoor work like Kate did was crucial to the smooth operation of the family, but my memories are of my role in the outside farm work. Most of that work differed by the seasons, but from the time we were seven or eight my siblings and I were responsible for daily morning and evening chores. The cows were driven in from the pasture to be milked twice daily, and in preparation we bedded their stables with straw or corn fodder. Eggs were gathered daily, and all the animals were fed and watered twice daily. With rare exceptions like illness, I helped with these same tasks on the same morning and evening schedule seven days a week, 52 weeks a year until I left home to attend college.

To milk the cows, we chased them into a large stable that had a manger with stanchions along the inside. We placed ground grain feed in the manger, and when a cow stuck her head through a stanchion opening to get the feed we closed the stanchion on her neck. After milking the cow and pouring the milk through a strainer into a milk can, we opened the stanchion so the cow could get out of the stable and go back to the pasture. Once or twice in my memory we altered this approach and milked the cows in the pasture field. On these occasions, our creek flooded from heavy rains, and the cows were stranded in a part of the pasture that was cut off from the house and barn by the creek. Since we couldn't get the cows to the barn, we loaded our milking equipment on a wagon pulled by our tractor and drove along roads and across a bridge to get to the cows.

As for the seasonal work, winter was the least busy season. Dad took advantage of the slower winter pace to catch up on the maintenance of farm buildings and equipment for which he had little time during the other three seasons. Winter was also the time of year Jim and I spent many Saturdays helping Dad clean out the animal pens. We used pitch forks to load the manure mixed with straw or corn fodder bedding into the manure spreader and then spread it on fields that were to be planted in grain in the spring. This smelly job was not one of our favorites, but it was important. As my farmer friend, Oscar Jutte, said years later, manure being spread on the fields "is the smell of money."

Spring was the season for preparing the fields and planting the crops, with the exception of winter wheat. The wheat fields were plowed and tilled and the wheat planted in the fall early enough to allow the plants to emerge and grow several inches before the winter freeze. The wheat went dormant in the winter to re-emerge and continue growing in the spring. The weather in spring and throughout the growing season was an important variable in farm life.

If spring weather was too cold or too wet for too long, planting may have to be delayed to the point of hurting the crop yields. Yields could be hurt if the weather was too dry or too hot during the planting and growing seasons. Heavy rains or severe windstorms at any time during the growing season may damage the crops. Too much rain at harvest time could delay the harvest past the point of maximum crop yield. Rain on a mowed field of hay might hurt the hay's quality. With so much at stake, we listened carefully and often to weather reports and watched the sky for signs of what weather to expect in the coming hours and days. I still enjoy watching cloud formations and storm development, as I am reminded of my youth on the farm.

The work associated with growing and harvesting the crops was completed with few breaks throughout the summer and into November. In June, corn was cultivated two or three times as it grew from a few inches to a foot or so in height. The first mowing of hay usually came in June with one or two more in the next two months. Wheat and oats were harvested in late June or early July. Soybeans were combined in September or early October. Corn was picked in October or early November, and then we were back full circle to preparing and planting the winter wheat fields. This cycle was repeated year after year on the Schoen farm.

I have fond memories of the sorghum harvest in the fall. Ripe sorghum, which we called sugar cane, looked like a shorter version of corn with no ears and a broom-like top of black seeds. The inside of the stalk was sweet and tasty. When it was ready, we stripped the leaves from the sorghum stalks by hitting down on them with wooden laths, then topped and cut the stalks with corn knives to be bundled and loaded on our farm wagon.

With the tractor, we took the wagonload of sorghum about twelve miles to a processing plant where it was made into molasses. The tractor ride took about an hour each way, and Dad allowed some of us kids to ride along on the wagon. That was always a fun ride, and from the time I was thirteen I was allowed to drive the tractor. I liked the sweet sorghum molasses as a spread for bread, and Dad loved it. A special treat for him was to soak a slice of bread in bacon grease and spread molasses over that.

* * *

Until the late 1940s, we had two workhorses to help with the farm work. When I was six or seven years old, Dad and Grandpa taught me how to harness the horses, hitch them to a wagon, a plow and other farm implements, handle their reins, and use verbal signals—"gee" for a right turn and "haw" for a left turn. (There was a popular song in the late 1950s whose lyrics had those directions reversed, that is, "...you turn to the left when I say gee; you turn to the right when I say haw." The reversal confused me at first, but I later learned the performers who sang the song were from England where the meanings of these commands are, in actual practice, reversed.)

We used a horse to operate the hay fork that ran on a rope and pulley system to take large stacks of hay from a wagon parked on the barn's thresh floor up into the haymow. I began to help with the hay in one of the last years we had workhorses, 1948 or 1949. Dad or Grandpa worked on the hay wagon, while the other was stationed in the haymow. When the man on the wagon finished setting the hayfork's prongs into the hay, he signaled to me.

My job was to walk behind our workhorse, Babe, and handle her reins as she pulled the hay rope at an angle away from the barn. When the forkful of hay reached the trolley at the top of the barn, it ran across the track above the haymow. The man working there yelled to the wagon man to pull the trip rope when the hay was where he wanted it. When I heard the fork trip and the hay fall into the mow, I stopped Babe and unhooked the rope so the fork could be pulled back to the wagon. I then guided Babe back to the barn and re-attached her to the rope for the next fork load of hay.

The work was mostly repetitious and routine, but I got a memorable scare on one fork load. As the hay rope became taut behind Babe, I realized she was veering from her usual path and toward her stable around the far corner of the barn. I anxiously yelled "haw! haw! haw!" as I pulled on her left rein, but to no avail. I was walking between the taut rope and the barn, so as Babe went around the corner of the barn my neck was pinned between the rope and the barn. I panicked and began to yell at the top of my lungs.

Trolley for a hay fork   Hay fork prongs

Fortunately, the surface of the old barn was not perfectly flat, to say the least, and I was standing at an indentation where there was barely enough space for my neck between the rope and the side of the barn. Once the fork reached the top of the barn and began its run across the haymow on the trolley, there was plenty of slack in the rope for me to escape. On the hay wagon, Dad heard my histrionics and came running. He grabbed Babe's reins as she was pawing at her stable door at the front of the barn. She did not respond to my commands because her left rein was worn through. Cooperative and hard working as Babe was, she was also tired and hungry, so with no reins directing her to do otherwise she decided to go home for some food and rest.

In the last few years that we had workhorses, we also had a ten- or fifteen-year-old Farmall tractor with steel wheels. It soon became clear plowing and most fieldwork could be done more efficiently and economically with the tractor. Gasoline was expensive, but the tractor used it only when operating. The horses had to eat regularly no matter how little they were used. Economic advantages or not, after a lifetime of farming with horses it was difficult for Grandpa Schoen to give them up.

After Dad sold the workhorses, he decided to buy a newer tractor, a Case SC with rubber tires. I was excited about getting the Case, because I had never been able to drive the Farmall. Its clutch was too far away for me to operate it with my foot. When the Case arrived, I jumped up on the seat and reached for the foot pedal on the right I assumed to be the clutch. I could reach it with ease, but when I pushed as hard as I could it hardly budged.

Seeing my disappointment, Dad smiled and pointed out I had pushed on a foot brake. The Case had a hand-operated clutch, and I could operate it efficiently. It was a joyful moment for me, but I didn't foresee it marked the beginning of thousands of hours over the next ten or twelve years behind the wheel of the Case—hauling manure, plowing, tilling, planting, cultivating corn, mowing, tedding and side-raking hay, mowing grain stubbles, baling straw and hay, loading loose hay, moving wagon-loads of grain, hay and straw, and on and on.

* * *

Through the 1940s, harvesting wheat or oats was a multi-step and time-consuming task on our farm. When the grain was ripe, it was cut and bound into twine-tied bundles using a horse- or tractor-drawn automatic binder. After the grain was cut, we walked

Field with wheat shocks

around the field, collecting and stacking the bundles in shocks to dry. After a few sunny days in shocks, the grain bundles were dry enough for threshing.

Dad and Mom were members of a group of neighbors who helped each other with their threshing. I don't remember everyone in our threshing ring, but it included Dad's brother Lee and his wife Sophia who was called Tubby. A year younger than me, Harry and Jerry, Lee and Tubby's twin sons, and Jim and I were inseparable playmates through elementary school. We were too young to help with the work, so threshing (we said

31

"thrashing") days at our farm and at theirs, a mile west of ours, were great fun for us.

Al Staugler, Dad's bachelor first cousin, who lived less than a mile away, owned and operated the steam tractor and threshing machine for our ring. On the morning of threshing day, we watched eagerly for the tractor and thresher to begin creeping along on its 15- or 20-minute trip from Al's farm to the corner of our "home road," the Mercer/Darke county line, and then the remaining half mile to our farm. After the thresher was positioned in our barnyard and connected by a long leather belt to the steam tractor's power take-off, it was ready for the wheat or oats.

The men used three or four horse- or tractor-drawn wagons to bring the grain from the field to the barnyard. Each filled wagon was pulled beside the thresher where men on the wagon used pitchforks to toss the grain bundles

Threshing machine pulled by steam tractor

into the threshing machine. The thresher separated the grain from the straw and blew the straw onto a large stack in the cow yard beside our barn. It was used for bedding the cow and horse stables through the next year.

The noise of the operating machinery and bustle of activity were exciting for us kids. We enjoyed watching the straw accumulate in a stack as it was blown out of the thresher. Chaff and dust were thick in the air, blown by even the slightest breeze, to eventually settle on the ground and vegetation around our barnyard. As the day wore on, a continuous layer of chaff several inches thick formed.

In one of the last years we threshed, Harry, Jerry, Jim, and I were running, playing, and having a great time unaware the chaff and dust had completely covered a wallowing hole in the hog field just across the fence from the cow yard. Poor Jim ran right into the hole and fell "splat" face down into a foot or so of wet mud and came up nearly covered from head to toe with the stuff.

While the men were working outside, the women were busy preparing food in the house. This included a morning and afternoon lunch at about ten a.m. and three p.m. The morning lunch may be cookies or coffee cake with coffee to drink, with meat and cheese sandwiches and lemonade more common in the afternoon. We kids brought the lunches to the men at work in the fields or on the threshing machine.

At noon, Al Staugler blew the whistle on the steam tractor to let everyone know it was time for dinner. Before dinner, the women had heated buckets of water on the kitchen stove. They poured the warm water into basins set up on a table in the shade near the house so the men could wash off the dust and dirt before sitting down to eat. Fried chicken, beef and gravy, pork chops, or Swiss steak were typical meats served for dinner accompanied by sliced tomatoes, mashed potatoes and gravy, corn and all sorts of garden vegetables, biscuits or bread with butter, jelly or jam, and, for dessert, pie, cake, or pudding. The women and kids ate after the men were finished.

By the time all of our wheat and oats was threshed, the straw stack was 15 to 20 feet high and filled most of the cow yard. Following threshing, the straw was loosely packed so we sank into it if we climbed on the stack. But after a week or two of scttling, the stack was solid enough for us to climb and play on it. Just climbing up and sliding down was fun for a while. We also played "king of the hill" where we teamed up and tried to capture and maintain the top of the straw stack by pushing those on the other team off when they attacked. The straw stack was also great for playing cowboys, as we imagined it to be a mountain where our cowboy heroes rode their horses as they pursued outlaws in the old west.

Farmers stopped threshing and threshing rings disbanded when it became much more efficient to combine the grain. Combines cut the grain and separated it from the straw at the same time. The separated grain accumulated in the combine's bin and the straw was dumped continuously out the back of the combine as it went around the field. Each time the grain bin filled, the grain was transferred into a wagon or truck bed using an auger. The straw was bailed a few days to a week after combining. By the early 1950s, large self-propelled combines were commonly used in grain fields in Mercer and Darke County, and threshing machines and giant stacks of loose straw became part of farming history.

* * *

Threshing rings were just one example of how farmers helped their neighbors and received help from them in return. In early May 1955, a small tornado hit our farm and that of neighbor, Clarence Weitzel, whose farm was directly across County Line Road. As Pat reminded me, the tornado hit on the Sunday of Doris's First Communion and my Solemn Communion, a church ritual marking graduation from elementary school. Damage to our buildings was minor. Some shingles were blown off our house and the garage roof collapsed on top of our car, but to me the most striking storm casualty on our farm was our cherry tree. The tightly rotating wind split the tree vertically in half the length of the trunk. One half remained standing, and the other half was flattened to the ground. The Weitzels were not as fortunate. Their large bank barn remained standing, but it sustained severe damage to its wooden siding and metal roof.

Farmers in the area had little or no insurance for such damage. Instead after the damage was assessed and a local lumberyard helped plan for repairs, all the neighbors pitched in to provide the labor, tools, and materials for the repairs. For several days, the Weitzel barnyard was teeming with activity as many of their neighbors came to help raise new beams, fix siding, and repair the roof.

Neighbors often worked together on tasks that were too large or complex to be completed by an individual farmer. Tony Homan, one mile east of us, had ten or fifteen acres of woods. He cut firewood for his family from his woods each fall and winter, but he needed help to do it. Dad agreed to work with him in exchange for enough wood for our winter fuel. I helped, too, along with Tony's son Gerald who was two years older than me. Tony, with Dad's advice, decided which trees to cut down. We used iron wedges and a cross-cut saw to cut a tree down while directing its fall to an open area.

After the tree was down, we all worked at cutting it into manageable-sized logs. After we had enough wood in the form of logs, we used a "buzz saw" hooked to a tractor power take-off by a long leather belt to cut the logs into firewood. I remember Dad pointing out that a belt with a half-twist wore evenly on both sides. Later in graduate school when our Topology class studied Moebius strips, some of my classmates were pretty confused about how they could be one-sided, but for me they were like our buzz-saw belt with a half twist.

Similar to the communal approach to threshing in the summer, neighbors formed rings for butchering hogs in the winter. Each winter through the 1950s, we butchered four or five of our fattened hogs with the help of our neighbors and helped them do the same. Butchering was deliberately scheduled on cold days to provide natural refrigeration for the meat.

Perhaps because of the cold and the fact I was old enough to help by the mid-fifties, my memories of butchering days are not as pleasant as those of threshing days. The work schedule for butchering days was similar to threshing, and the food was good.

We liked to eat the cracklings, the greasy skins left over from rendering the lard. Dinner always included some of the newly butchered cuts of pork.

In the week or two after butchering, we ate blood pudding and the hogs' livers and sweetbreads (pancreas). I loved all three, especially the sweetbreads. The hearts, brains and tongues were also used, I think, by being ground and put into the blood pudding. The head meat was ground and combined with pin oats and spices to make German grits that we ate for breakfast. The sausage meat was ground, seasoned, and stuffed into the hogs' cleaned intestinal linings then cut into links. Mom canned the sausage in glass jars that were then stored on a shelf in our cool, moist cellar.

Before we had a refrigerator or freezer, we cured the hams, bacons and shoulders in salt brine with bones intact and hung them from the ceiling above the stairs to the cellar. When Mom decided to make a pork meal, she took down a ham, bacon or shoulder and sliced off as much as she needed, then hung the bone with its reduced meat content back in the cellar.

Cooking apple butter was another communal activity, mainly for the women. Mom's apple butter group was made up of her mother and one or two of her sisters and sisters-in-law. They all came over to our house on the agreed upon day. In the morning, they prepared the apples they had brought and those we had gathered from our orchard adding the sugar and spices needed for apple butter. Of course, this was all accompanied by lots of socializing and good food.

A large copper pot holding 15 or 20 gallons was used. I can't remember if we owned the pot or someone else brought it, but it was placed in the shade under our gigantic cottonwood tree just across the fence from the barnyard. Dad built a wood fire under the pot, timed to be just hot enough when the apples were ready to be cooked. The apple mix was put into the pot where it cooked on the fire for two or more hours. The women then strained and canned the apple butter and divided it among themselves.

* * *

Ed Kemper was one of my best friends. Our friendship began in high school as classmates and teammates in sports and deepened when I was an undergraduate rooming in Dayton for three summers with Ed and his older brother Dick, among one or two others. Once on a car trip home for a weekend, Ed, Dick, and I were joking around about our families when Dick referred to my Dad as "The Bright Spark in Darke." We thought that was clever and laughed a lot at the time. Ed or I sometimes brought the name up when we were together in later years just to laugh all over again.

In fact, Dad had his faults but he was a spark in my life, particularly through elementary school. Some of his faults were small ones like being overly impatient when I held the flashlight for him as he worked in the dark on some emergency fix-it
Dad and Jim in 1957

job. Other faults were more serious including some bad judgments concerning family finances and a heavy cigarette smoking habit that caused his death at 82 from emphysema.

Dad had little financial success as a farmer, but he had a penchant for inventing useful gadgets. For example, near the fence line between the house yard and barnyard was a large black walnut tree that produced hundreds of walnuts each autumn. Common in the area, the black walnuts were delicious but the edible part was not easy to access. A black walnut has a thick soft green outer shell that covers the hard inner shell in which the edible part of the nut is encased.

The outer shells are easy to remove but they have a juicy substance inside that produces a deep brown stain on hands and anything else it touches. The stain resists soap and hot water. When I was in elementary school, its effects were often visible for a week or more on my hands and those of my peers. The inner shell is difficult to remove. Nutcrackers sturdy enough to crack English walnuts or pecans are useless for these hard shells. Placing the nut on an anvil or brick and hitting it hard with a hammer cracks the shell, but it often smashes the edible part of the nut to a pulp.

One fall, Dad decided to apply his inventive skills to the double problem of finding a stain-free method to remove the outer black walnut shells and a way to remove the inner shells that left the edible nut meat largely intact. Starting with his usual "Let's see what we can accomplish," Dad designed and built a trough-like sheller that was slightly more than the width of a rear tire of our car. It was rounded upward on either end, was about 6 inches high in the middle, and had a metal bottom. Dad jacked a rear wheel of the car up off the ground and fit the sheller under the tire and around its bottom part. He then dropped the wheel to about an inch above the bottom of the sheller.

When the car was started, put into first gear, and the transmission engaged, the wheel suspended inside the sheller rotated. The rotating wheel was just high enough above the bottom of the sheller that when we fed black walnuts into the sheller from the front of the tire their outer shells were squashed under the tire leaving only their inner shells intact. The nuts were forced by the rotating tire out the rear of the sheller onto a rectangular piece of plywood. With a stick, we separated the walnuts on the plywood to form a single layer with no two nuts touching; then left them to dry for a few days.

Dad's idea for cracking the inner shells once the nuts were dry was to use a screw mechanism like a vice to increase the pressure slowly on the inner nutshell until it cracked. This method did not guarantee the nut's entire edible insides survived in one piece, but it was more effective than our hammer and anvil technique. To make this work, Dad built a sturdy wooden box about 6 inches high with roughly an 8-inch square bottom but no top. At the top of the box, he mounted a vice-like screw apparatus that opened a little wider than a black walnut with no outer shell. Once a nut was cracked in the vice, the pieces of shell and nut meat fell down into the box where they could be easily accessed for further separation of broken shell and edible nut.

For a man with little formal education, Dad's intuition about mathematical ideas was impressive. Conversions of measurement units, the use of pi in the area and circumference of a circle, estimating heights of trees by measuring the lengths of the shadows of a

Elevated gasoline tank for farm use

fence post and the tree, and estimating areas of irregularly shaped regions were all within Dad's comfort zone.

On one occasion, I was at home for a weekend during my sophomore year in college when Dad posed a problem he hoped I could solve using the calculus I was learning. In our barnyard, we had an elevated tank to store gasoline. It was similar to the one pictured. Every month a large fuel truck stopped to replenish the supply in the tank by pumping gasoline through the circular door opening at the top.

Dad wondered how to calibrate a dipstick to measure the number of gallons of gasoline in the tank when the stick was pushed to the bottom of the tank through the opening at the top. He knew the consecutive marks on the stick would not be the same distance apart but wasn't sure how to place them. The solution does not require calculus, but I found the problem to be interesting and challenging. I was surprised Dad was able to state it so well.

On another occasion, Dad's independent thinking was a handicap. The New Idea Manufacturing Company in Coldwater produced manure spreaders. After World War II, business was booming, and many local farmers decided to apply for jobs. They could earn union wages, have health care coverage, a pension plan and still operate their farms or rent the fields to other area farmers for a share of the crop. Since we were barely getting by on our farm, Dad decided to apply at "the spreader works," too. He was hired to work second shift, arriving at work at 4:30 or 5:00 pm and working until after midnight. To relieve Dad of some of the farm work, he and Mom rented several of our fields to a farmer neighbor.

During the year or so Dad worked at New Idea, the family's financial restrictions eased up. With the factory pay and the farm profits, this was the most regular income Dad ever made. Mom and Dad also used New Idea's medical insurance to have Mom's goiter on the side of her neck removed and to pay for my brother Rick's birth. Renting the fields was not without its problems, though, as one summer morning Mom and the neighbor who was renting some of our land had a heated argument. Mom thought he had taken more of the crop than their agreement called for, and she was letting him know as much in no uncertain terms. Embarrassed by Mom's outburst, Dad was trying to smooth things over.

I'm not sure how that controversy was settled, but Dad hated his job at the New Idea from the start. He didn't respond well to the factory environment and disliked not being "his own boss" as he was on the farm. Mom was never comfortable being home alone at night, so she didn't protest loudly when, in spite of the medical insurance and relatively high wages, Dad quit his job at New Idea and went back to working the entire farm. Unfortunately, he wrote a letter to the New Idea management protesting that he was owed more "back pay"; retirement contributions he made during his time on the job. In a few years, financial problems again became pressing, and, at Mom's urging, Dad reapplied for a job at New Idea. This time he wasn't hired, because "they did not like his attitude about back pay."

When I was a little kid, I was in awe of Dad's physical stamina and strength, and so the few times I saw him in vulnerable situations were scary and memorable to me. Once he was in the barn working on the corn picker, and I was there to hand him tools he needed. The corn picker, Grandpa and Dad's junkyard special, had two wheels in the rear, but much of the weight of the rollers and other parts that picked the corn was on the front tongue of the picker.

This day Dad needed to repair something located under the front end of the picker. To do the repair, he placed the end of the tongue on a large piece of firewood stood on end and crawled on his back under the tongue and the front of the picker. He worked a while in that position, but at some point he bumped too hard against the tongue and it slipped off the firewood. Dad was on his back on the ground and struggling hard to hold the heavy tongue up away from him.

At eight or ten years old, I couldn't lift the tongue myself so I didn't know what to do. With signs of panic and physical strain in his voice, Dad directed me to set the firewood up next to the end of the tongue. Then the two of us lifting together set the tongue back on the firewood so Dad could get out from under. Telling Mom about the incident that evening, Dad said he was glad I was there and he didn't know what he would have done without my help. I beamed with pride to hear such rare praise from him.

Dad owned a .22 caliber rifle and a double-barreled shotgun he, and later my brothers and I, used for hunting rabbits in the winter. He hung these guns, always unloaded, on nails on the wall of the slop-bucket pantry. Before I was old enough to use the guns, I was curious about them. One day when no adults were around, Jim and I stood on a chair and lifted the rifle off the wall. We didn't know how to use it but we played around with it, being careful not to point it at anyone as Dad had taught us. After a while, we put it back on the wall and went on to some other activities.

A few days later, Dad decided to go hunting. He got the rifle down and was standing in the kitchen when he pulled the trigger. To everyone's shock the gun went off sending a bullet through the ceiling. When Jim and I were playing with the rifle I had unknowingly loaded a bullet into its chamber. I never saw Dad more shaken. He went out of the house, I think to the barn, for a half hour or more by himself to regain his composure. I was shaken, too, at the prospect of what could have happened had someone in the family been in the path of that bullet.

Throughout my childhood, Dad's health was good but one incident gave me a serious scare. To make it worse, it happened a week or two after Walter Sutter died of a heart attack. Like Dad, he was in his mid-forties and the father of a large family. Many of the Sutter kids were close in age to my siblings and me. They lived on a farm a couple of miles from ours, went to Sharpsburg Elementary and then Fort Recovery High like us, and we enjoyed playing softball with them. When their father died, we were very sad for them as we could envision ourselves in their situation.

One night, we were sitting in the dining room listening to the radio, reading, or playing as we did most evenings. Suddenly, Dad slipped out of his easy chair onto the floor and shook spastically as if he was having an epileptic fit. After a minute or so, he calmed down and seemed better, but he didn't remember what had happened. We kids were shocked and scared that, like the Sutters, we may soon end up without a father. Mom was worried, too, and she insisted Dad go see Doc Heurkamp in Fort Recovery the next day. Doc didn't find anything wrong. He concluded Dad was suffering from exhaustion, as we were in the midst of grain harvest season. Whether or not the doctor was right, Dad never had another seizure like that one.

* * *

For a number of years in the Spring, some of my siblings and I sold flower and vegetable seeds to neighbors and relatives. For our effort, we could choose from a catalogue of "swell prizes." One spring I chose a basketball for my prize, the first I ever owned. I was glad to have the ball, but when it arrived in the mail it was an inch smaller than regulation size, and it was an old-fashioned basketball then going out of style. Rather than a one-piece rubber-covered ball, its inside was rubber and, like a bicycle tire inner tube, held the air. The outer cover was leather or imitation leather. The inner ball was inserted into the cover through a slit that was closed with plastic laces before the ball was inflated.

One year, Dad found some gaps in several rows in the middle of our cornfield. He invited the kids who were old enough to plant pickles in those vacant sections of rows. We got excited about the project. We enjoyed trekking through the corn, planting the pickles carefully, weeding them, and, protected from view by the tall corn, keeping a close eye on our crop.

The weather must have been just right for pickles that year because we had a bumper crop. After Mom canned all the pickles she needed for our family, we put the remainder in bags, boxes and baskets and sold them to anyone who was interested. We had fun with our pickles and came away with a little money for each of us as well. As a musical theme of our project, we revised the lyrics of a popular song, substituting "pickles" for "music" in "All I want is loving you, and Music! Music! Music!"

For a couple of years, Dad contracted with Stemley's Cannery, located near New Weston, to raise ten or fifteen acres of tomatoes on our farm. The cannery provided the tractor-drawn tomato planter and plants, but we prepared the field and did the planting. Two kids rode on the back of the planter, one over each of the two rows the planter cut in the ground. When the planter automatically poured out a small cup of water and some fertilizer, we dropped a plant and a wheel tucked it in with dirt.

When the tomatoes were ripe, Stemley's provided Hispanic itinerant workers to do the picking. My siblings and I were also allowed to pick as much as we could and were paid at the going rate per hamper. I think it was around 25 cents. Many of the Hispanic workers could not speak English and were different from us culturally, but they were very efficient at picking tomatoes in contrast to our snail's pace. I made a little money but it was the hardest and least rewarding work I ever did. For years, their association in my mind with hot, backbreaking work ruined my appetite for tomatoes.

By the time I was in fifth or sixth grade, I worked occasionally for neighbors who needed temporary help. One of my first jobs was catching chickens for 25 cents an hour, but most of my work involved helping farmers with straw or hay baling usually for 50 cents an hour up to $1.00 as I got older. Lee Staugler, Al's brother whose farm adjoined Al's on the south, hired me to help him bale his straw a few summers starting when I was about 13.

One baling day at Stauglers, Lee's wife Mary served a dinner worthy of the old threshing day meals–fried chicken, several vegetables, and mashed potatoes and gravy, always a favorite of mine. I loaded my plate with a serving of everything, including a supersized helping of mashed potatoes with two large spoonsful of gravy. The chicken was delicious, but when I dug into the potatoes I noticed on the first forkful the gravy was strangely cold.

On the second forkful, I realized I had mistaken the butterscotch pudding for gravy. I looked up sheepishly but was too shy to say anything. Mary noticed my mistake, but I guess she was too polite to point it out so I ate my entire serving of butterscotch flavored mashed potatoes. It was an unusual combination of tastes. Later, Mary told Mom about my mistake, and everyone had a good laugh at my expense.

The work I describe in this chapter may sound like a lot, but the 137-acre farm was not large compared to many in the area so the jobs could be completed pretty quickly. Our farm became even smaller in 1952 when I was in sixth grade. To cover debts, Mom and Dad sold the back 40 acres to our neighbor, Al Wendel. So even with hired work and my regular chores on our farm, I found time for reading, sports and other forms of recreation and play.

3 PLAY

The farm was not just a site for work, but also a giant playground for us kids when we had leisure time. Like town kids, we could play in our house and in the yard surrounding it. In addition we had exclusive access to a large barnyard, fruit orchard, the barn and other farm buildings, and 135 acres of fields that included a small woods and creek. Our creek was the Wabash River, a few miles from its source. Some of our play required large portions of the farm.

For example, when the corn was reaching its full height but was still fresh and green, we played tag and hide-and-seek in the cornfields, running full speed along the cornrows and skipping from row to row to escape being tagged by our playmates. In the winter, we sledded, skated with no skates on the frozen creek, built snow forts for snowball fights, made intertwining sets of tracks in the snow that covered the entire barnyard for a version of tag we called "fox and geese," and played many games in the barn. When we were old enough for *Red Ryder* air rifles, we used them to shoot sparrows asleep at night under the roof of the barn and other farm buildings.

When I was ten to twelve, Dad sometimes took me rabbit hunting on a winter Saturday. Later Jim and I hunted together.

Dan in 1964 with tractor shed and chicken coop in the background.

The rabbits sat in long grass or among bent cornstalks, so fencerows, pastures with long grass, and fields with picked corn were the best places to hunt. When we shot a rabbit, we twisted off its head and put it in a sack carried around our shoulders. Dad skinned and gutted the rabbits, and Mom cooked them for family meals.

Occasionally on a Sunday afternoon in the summer we went fishing in our creek, catching a few small catfish if we were lucky. Dad also trapped along the creek in the winter for a number of years, and I went with him regularly. It was best to trap when there was snow on the ground. Walking along the creek in the daytime, we could see where animals, mainly muskrats or raccoons, slid down the bank of the creek into the water. We set a trap just under the water's surface at the bottom of each slide.

Starting around four o'clock the next morning so we could be finished in time to do the feeding and milking, the two of us put on our heavy winter clothes including high-top boots and went out to check the traps. We may have ten or 15 muskrats or raccoons in our traps on any given morning. We also found traps

48

that were sprung but empty or contained a foot an animal chewed off to escape from the trap. A muskrat or raccoon skin was worth 25 to 50 cents, but once or twice we caught a mink that sold for around $20.

With the exception of fishing, hunting and trapping, we kids were entirely on our own when it came to sports and other play. There were no adult-operated Little League baseball or soccer teams for kids. In fact, we knew nothing about soccer. The adults did not organize any play for us until inter-school softball in sixth grade. Even when I was in high school and college, basketball players were not allowed to compete on a coached team outside the regular school or college schedule. The intent was to ensure basketball remained a fun game and did not become an obsession for the players. Of course, college basketball was not yet the huge and lucrative business it later became.

* * *

The woods and creek were great for playing cowboys and Indians, one of my favorite activities before age eight or nine. My playmates in those days were usually a few of my brothers and sisters, always including Jim, and sometimes my cousins, Harry and Jerry Schoen. For a few years beginning when I was in third or fourth grade, we had some more cousins nearby to play with. Mom's brother Al Heitkamp, his wife Edna, and their five children rented a farmhouse less than a mile east of us.

Pat was my age, a real tomboy who loved playing cowboys, Larry was one year younger, and Denny was two years younger than Larry. Riding imaginary horses (wooden broom handles) through the wilds of our woods and along the edge of the creek as we wielded our toy six-shooters and mouthed the sound of shots, the woods and creek stoked our imaginations in a way I think is captured by this excerpt from the introduction to *The*

Lone Ranger radio show, "Return with us now to those thrilling days of yesteryear, when out of the pass come the thundering hoof beats of the great horse, Silver! Hi Yo, Silver, awa-a-ay!"

The Heitkamps shook up our orderly, predictable imaginary world a bit. We often played with them in a new location we called the "tunnel," a large culvert that went under the road where Cochran Road dead-ends on the Mercer-Darke County Line Road. The tunnel was between our house and the Heitkamps', a little closer to them, and it was great as a hideout for bad guys or a site for an ambush.

My sister Pat commented, "When my kids were little I took them for a drive around our old neighborhood and shared some of my memories of growing up. When I told them about the tunnel and playing there they said, 'Boy, Mom you were so lucky!' I guess I was."

We had some disagreements on favorite cowboys. We all agreed the Lone Ranger and Hopalong Cassidy were cool, but Jim and I had always liked Gene Autry better than Roy Rogers, who we thought was something of a braggart for claiming to be "King of the Cowboys." Harry and Jerry agreed with us but to our chagrin, Larry was a died-in-the-wool fan of Roy's, and we had many arguments about that continuing, good naturedly, at family events to the present day.

Furthermore, Pat Heitkamp took the unconventional position of being a devoted fan of teen-aged cowboy Bobby Benson from *Bobby Benson & the B-Bar-B Riders*, a Saturday morning radio show for kids. To the rest of us, Bobby was OK but surely not on a par with Gene, Roy, or Hoppy. This didn't stop Pat from pretending to be Bobby Benson when we played, even to the point of trying to throw me over her shoulder in an imaginary fight like we all had seen in cowboy movies. This move didn't go far as I was five or six inches taller and 15 or 20 pounds heavier.

Jim remembers playing the part of Windy Wales, a ranch

hand whose role on the show was to provide comic relief. I learned from the internet that on the *B-Bar-B* show Windy Wales was played by a young Don Knotts, who later became famous on television as deputy sheriff Barney Fife in the long running *Andy Griffith Show*.

I think it was Pat Heitkamp's idea to have a long-distance signal to summon us to their house. She and her brothers in unison would yell "mabe" (pronounced maybe), a supposed Indian word for "attack" from the *B-Bar-B* show. When we heard this yell, we were to rush to their house. I don't remember ever using this signal, possibly because we couldn't hear them yelling, if they ever did, from nearly a mile away,

The winding creek with its overgrown banks where we trapped muskrats and played cowboys and Indians was on the 40 acres Mom and Dad sold to Al Wendel in 1952. One of the first things Al did after taking ownership was straighten and dredge the creek so it no longer flooded. By doing so, he improved the productivity of the land but took away all that made the creek so much fun for kids.

* * *

Harry, Jerry, and the Al Heitkamp children were the first cousins we played with most, but we saw many of our cousins a few times a year when our families visited or we had parties for special family events. Since we didn't know these cousins well, there was an awkward "getting re-acquainted" time at first, but shortly into the visit we began to have fun with the cousins near us in age.

A memorable event on Dad's side of the family was his parents' fiftieth wedding anniversary in 1951. Grandpa and Grandma celebrated it with a huge party in Sharpsburg that was based at their house, but we played with my siblings and cousins at the school playground, the baseball field, and all over town.

My aunts, uncles and first cousins on the Schoen side in 1951 including our family; Mom's side was similar in number. I am sitting in the first row in front of Grandpa Schoen. Harry and Jerry are to my right.

* * *

On rainy days and on winter weekends, we often played in the barn. What follows is a sentimental remembrance of playing in the barn at age 10 that I wrote in 1971 at age 30. The specific memories are not as clear to me in my seventies, but the sentiments still feel right.

It was one of those dreary, rain-splattered summer days that causes sinking feelings in the hearts of all kids. Not that the crops didn't need the moisture. We were all well aware of that. The weather governed our lives as it does that of all farm families. But for me at age ten, being forced to stay indoors was a fate worse than any drought.

As much as we kids dreaded such days, Mom must have a hundred times more, for there were ten of us, ranging from one to 17 years of age. On this particular day, we had been out of bed, and in usual vocal form for an hour when Mom convinced us there was fun to be had in the barn. Off the middle kids went, running through the rain. The three big kids could not at 14, 15 and 17, seem to get enthused over the joys the barn could offer. Nor did the two little kids join us, though they would in time take part in such ventures. For the present, we couldn't let them slow us down as we had a full schedule of activities ahead in that big, beautiful barn.

The barn, twenty years later, looks much the same as it did then though a little more rundown. Now it is big, but far from beautiful. The roof leaks; the paint is nearly all peeled off; most of the doors cannot be opened by anything short of a battering ram. It is used only for storage of machinery. Then it was the next thing to Heaven for us kids; a place to live in our own

Dave sledding in the barnyard in 1964

fantasy world. Here there were no adults to tell us to be quiet. We were not laughed at or pushed around by the big kids nor were the little kids destroying our prized possessions.

Inside the barn door a new world opened up to us. What to do? Should we build tunnels in the straw bales with sharp curves, varying heights and multiple levels? Or would it be more fun today to build forts and choose sides for a corn-cob fight? How about hide-and-seek? The hay and straw mows, granary, and farm machinery offered many creative hiding places. Or we could play "king of the hill" on the haystack. These games, with their many variations and combinations, are just a sample of the wide assortment of possibilities. In the course of the morning, we tried several; each, in its duration, a pure delight.

All too soon we heard Mom calling us to the house for dinner, *the noon meal. To our surprise the rain had stopped, and, we knew as we trudged to the house, so had our fun in the barn for that day.*

Dad and Mom sold the farm in 1967 and retired to what had been Grandpa and Grandma Schoen's house in Sharpsburg. To Mom's great sorrow, the new owner of the farm burned down the house shortly after he bought the farm. He used some of the other buildings including the barn to store machinery until the mid-1970s when he tore down the remaining buildings.

* * *

Each weekday evening during my early elementary school years after the animals were fed and the cows were milked, around 7:00 pm, the entire family listened to the radio for an hour. We all liked comedy and mystery shows, and the boys loved westerns and super-hero stories, too.

At 8:00 we got ready for bed so we could get up early the next morning to do our chores, which for me were to milk two or three cows by hand, before catching the school bus. An exception to that schedule was on Thursday nights when we were allowed to stay up an extra hour to listen to our two favorite family comedies, *Father Knows Best* and *The Aldrich Family*.

Many of the radio shows had distinctive openings, and some had classical music in the background. I still get the urge to mount a horse and gallop off into the sunset yelling "Hi Yo, Silver, Away" when I hear the William Tell Overture, the theme music of *The Lone Ranger* show. Memories of the *Green Hornet* and his crime-fighting pal Kato come to my mind when I hear the Flight of the Bumblebee. And I vividly recall the opening for *Superman*, "Look! Up in the sky! It's a bird! It's a plane! It's Superman!"

Dad liked detective and crime shows on the radio, and there

were lots of them. *The Shadow* and *Inner Sanctum* were very scary with ominous openings I described in Chapter 1. J. Edgar Hoover, head of the FBI, used the radio to help shape public opinion about his bureau with two half hour crime shows: *This is Your FBI* and *Your FBI in Peace and War*. Other shows of this genre we often listened to included: *Gang Busters, Nick Carter - Master Detective, Sam Spade, Boston Blackie*, and *Mr. Keen, Tracer of Lost Persons*. Another, *The Fat Man*, was a detective character created by well-known writer Dashiell Hammett. Dad always laughed at the show's opening:

There he goes, into that drugstore.

He's stepping on the scales.

Weight: 239 pounds.

Fortune: Danger.

Who is it?

THE FAT MAN!!

There were also many radio shows for younger kids that were broadcast early on weekday evenings or on Saturday mornings. Some of our favorites were *Straight Arrow, Sky King, Fury*, and *Bobby Benson and the B-Bar-B Riders*. Mom and even Dad, though he did not like to admit it, enjoyed daytime radio soap operas like *Stella Dallas* and *Back-Stage Wife*. In fact, my sister Linda's name was partially prompted by a popular radio soap opera, *Linda's First Love*. Two of my younger brothers, Ricky and David, are namesakes of the sons of Ozzie Nelson and Harriet Hilliard of the popular family comedy *Ozzie & Harriet*.

The Nabisco Company sponsored the *Straight Arrow* radio show. It opened with the star of the show, supposedly an Indian, chanting loudly to a steady beating of drums:

N-A-B-I-S-C-O

Nabisco is the name to know.

For a breakfast you can't beat.

Try Nabisco Shredded Wheat.

Jim and I disliked Nabisco Shredded Wheat, but for a while

we ate it for breakfast so we could get the Straight Arrow "injun-uity" card that was in each box. Each injun-uity card gave directions for making a teepee, a tomahawk, a campfire or something else in keeping with stereotypes prevalent at the time about American Indians. We didn't usually make those things, but we enjoyed collecting the cards.

A favorite show of some of my sisters was *Your Hit Parade*, a prime-time Saturday night offering that featured the most famous singers of the day performing the previous week's top hit songs. Performers like Doris Day, Bing Crosby and Frank Sinatra all made appearances on the show. One song my sisters loved was *Tennessee Waltz* sung by Patti Page. When I was in elementary school, my favorite song was *Ghost Riders in the Sky* sung by several different singers including Burl Ives, Gene Autry, Vaughan Monroe, and Frankie Laine.

Bob Hope, Jack Benny, and George Burns & Gracie Allen all had comedy shows we loved. *Our Miss Brooks* starring comedienne Eve Arden and *The Life of Riley* with William Bendix were also among our favorites. As happened later in television, popular radio shows sometimes had spinoff shows based on one or more of the characters in the original show. An example I remember was the water commissioner, Throckmorton P. Gildersleeve, a regular character on the popular *Fibber McGee and Molly* show, who got his own comedy show, called *The Great Gildersleeve*. We liked both of those shows.

We got our first black-and-white television in 1956 or 1957 when I was in high school. With our rooftop antenna we could watch two blurry channels located 60 miles away in Dayton, one affiliated with NBC and the other with CBS. By then television had made the comedy and drama shows on radio nearly obsolete, although many of those radio shows were adapted for television in the 1950s. Having the television picture was an impressive technological breakthrough, but the old dramas and comedies were more fun for me on radio. Radio required you to listen actively and to use your imagination to picture what was going on.

The radio shows were fun, but we enjoyed other family activities in the evenings, on weekends, or on rainy summer days. When we were very young, Jim and I spent hours playing with cardboard boxes, cutting holes in them at different levels and making a coordinated sequence of chutes by folding up long narrow strips of cardboard and slipping them through the holes in the box. We placed marbles at the top of our chute system so they rolled from one chute to the next lower one eventually coming out at the bottom. We constructed the chute system so the path of the marbles was as complex as possible.

Card games were popular with the whole family. With the wide range of ages, it was common for the younger kids to be playing War, *Old Maid* or *Authors*, while the older kids and often Mom and Dad played Pepper (Bid Euchre), Pinochle, Hearts, or Sheepshead. We played board games for a range of ages as well; *Chutes & Ladders* and *Uncle Wiggily* for the little kids and *Monopoly*, *Clue*, and *Sorry* for the older ones. The wooden kitchen table with its two or three extension leaves wasn't long, wide, or smooth enough to be an official ping pong table, but we put up a net and played on it anyway.

A lively card game based on the commodities trading market called *Pit* was a favorite of ours for a while. This game had a lasting impact on Jim. He and his wife Mary Ann have for many years hosted an annual *Pit* party for their friends. One year, one of their friends gave Jim a pair of slippers – one is the bear and the other is the bull, as in the *Pit* game. As a result, his friends refer to him as the *Pit* Master.

When I was in early elementary school. Jim and I enjoyed a popular game called *Bas-ket* that was played with a pingpong ball on a cardboard court painted like a basketball court with a netted wire basket set up at each end that was large enough for the ping pong ball to go through comfortably. There were holes

 on the court at different shot locations, and under each hole was a spring-loaded lever. When the ball rolled into a hole, one of the players used a handle mounted on the side of the cardboard court to release the spring that projected the ball toward the basket. I remember one of us getting *Bas-ket* for Christmas several different times. It was a simple game but we enjoyed swishing the ball through the net, even if it was only a pingpong ball.

An important part of our evening entertainment was popcorn, a snack we all loved. We raised it ourselves in the truck garden across the lane from our house, so it was one of the few snack foods we could eat as much as we wanted. Dad was happy to let us kids take full responsibility for the popcorn crop, and we always raised plenty to last us until the next year's harvest.

Jim commented, "Do you remember the year we had a bumper crop of popcorn? I think we had 500 pounds of shelled popcorn. We were never able to finish all of it. We could have been like the Huck-a-Bucks." In a children's story by Carl Sandburg, the Huck-a-Buck family's farm buildings were all filled with popcorn they had stored for the winter until a fire popped it leaving the family struggling to keep their heads above mountains of popped corn.

* * *

It was in Fort Recovery where we first saw in the stores and sometimes bought comic books, big little books, and other popular books for children, as well as packs of bubble gum that contained pictures of major league baseball players. My older sisters liked books, and Ginny had collected a few popular books for young people. From their example, I began to love reading, starting with simple stories about cowboys and mysteries solved by kids.

We made regular use of the Fort Recovery Public Library, and there I discovered baseball history and biographies of famous people written for children. In the summer, when I had some time off from chores, I often grabbed a book or some comic books and climbed an apple tree for a private reading space sitting on a limb and leaning against the tree trunk.

Through Harry and Jerry, we began collecting cowboy and super-hero comic books. Their older brother Lester, four years older than me, had a collection from the early to mid-1940s he had outgrown. Les's collection included some of the earliest issues of our favorite superheroes, Batman, Superman, and Captain Marvel. He also had comic books about movie cowboys from an earlier era including Tom Mix, Buck Jones, and Ken Maynard. In good condition, many of those comic books would be valuable collectors' items today.

Unfortunately, ours didn't survive the passage of time. Jim and I didn't help with their survival, as our littler brothers and sisters were pretty destructive when they got their hands on them. Mom, in her efforts to keep the house neat and uncluttered, sometimes threw our comic books away if we left them lying around the house. To keep them safe from Mom and the little kids one winter, we built a roomy cave in the straw bales in the barn. We hid some of our most prized comic books in the cave. They were safe from our family members all right, but some barn rats found them and had a chewy meal. We solved that problem by making a wooden box that kept 25 or so comic books safe from the rats.

We didn't just collect and read these comic books. We

became trivia experts, knowing every superhero's secret identity and origin story and the name of every cowboy's horse. Once we named as many movie and comic book cowboys and their horses as we could. We stopped somewhere in the seventies.

Following and partially overlapping our comic book collecting, Harry, Jerry, Jim and I began to save baseball bubble gum trading cards. From 1903 to 1953, major league baseball consisted of the same 16 teams. Each of us collected players' cards from four of the teams. Some of our elementary school classmates also collected baseball cards, and we negotiated trades with them.

When any of the four of us bought baseball bubble gum or traded for a card, we gave the card to the brother or cousin who collected that player's team. We spent many hours together checking out each of the four collections, planning trading strategy, looking at the players' pictures, and poring over their personal information and baseball statistics on the backs of the cards.

We soon saw players' cards were not placed in the bubble gum packs at random. It was much easier to find multiple pictures of little known players than it was to find even one picture of the all-stars of the era. We had 40 or more pictures of an obscure pitcher named Marlin Stuart, but only one or two of Stan Musial, Ted Williams, Mickey Mantle, and Willie Mays.

In the 1970s, Jim passed our collection on to his sons, and I believe Harry and/or Jerry did the same with their cards. My sister Pat's sons had some of my cards, which they recently returned to me. We played too much with our cards to keep them in mint condition, so none are worth much even Mickey Mantle in his rookie year.

* * *

Most of the movies the family saw until the mid-1950s were

shown free each Saturday night in the summers on an outdoor screen in a gravel parking lot beside Harry Birt's grocery store in New Weston (1950 population – 136). They were usually westerns, comedies or mysteries that were ten or more years old, but we enjoyed them. Besides watching the movie, we liked to run around on the piles of gravel behind the screen. We could see the movie from the front or back of the screen, which was the thickness of a bed sheet. The wide variety of bulk candy and heaping ice cream cones Birt's sold for 5 or 10 cents added to our pleasure on those summer evenings.

Fort Recovery had a small indoor movie theater, the Royal Theater. I always loved indoor movies; almost any movie when I was young. The darkness of the theater with the moving images on the large screen provided a wonderful escape from reality. Before television, movies were so popular fans like us often entered theaters after the feature had begun, watched to the end, then watched the beginning to the point where we had come in when the movie was shown a second time. In later years, I became more selective both of the films I watch and my theater entry time, but I still feel a surge of escape when I enter a movie theater.

Until the early fifties, the Royal Theater showed movies nightly plus a Sunday matinee. For a few years thereafter, the Royal ran movies on weekends only. The theater finally closed in the late 1950s, although it continued for a year or two to re-open for a local tradition on the Saturday afternoon before Christmas – the showing of a free movie for children that gave their parents a chance to do some last-minute shopping in Fort Recovery stores. The movie was accompanied by the arrival of Santa on a Fort Recovery fire truck. One free Christmas movie I remember well was Charles Dickens' *A Christmas Carol*.

The family could rarely afford 15 to 25 cents each to see other movies at the Royal although Mom, Dad, or later one of my older sisters occasionally took the younger kids to a movie,

Royal Theater in early 1950s

usually a western starring Roy Rogers or Gene Autry or a comedy with Abbott & Costello or Martin & Lewis. In those days, "Short Subjects" were shown before the main feature including a newsreel of recent world news and a 15- or 20-minute comedy. Our favorite short comedies were *The Three Stooges* and their outrageous physical slapstick.

Two movies in the early fifties helped to spark my interest in basketball, *The Harlem Globetrotters* (1951) and *Go Man Go* (1954). Both were about the Harlem Globetrotters, a team of all black players, who then, and continuing to the present, put on a basketball show at arenas all over the world. The flashiness and comedy of the Globetrotters is pure showmanship, but in those days the Globetrotters were also capable of playing serious basketball on a par with top professional teams. I loved the basketball action in those movies. The Globetrotters' tricks were funny and often athletically impressive, but just the "swish" of the net when someone hit a shot was exciting to me.

In the summer, a crowded carload of Schoens sometimes paid

a dollar to attend Tuesday "buck" night at the Starlight Auto, a drive-in theater near Saint Henry. I remember seeing the 1950 movie *Cheaper by the Dozen* with my parents and many of my, at the time, nine or ten siblings and afterwards discussing the similarities and differences between the screen family and ourselves. We also saw many of the popular *Ma and Pa Kettle* series at the Starlight. Amazingly, the Starlight Auto continued to operate until 2012 or 2013. Bigger towns in the area like Portland, Coldwater, Celina and Greenville also had indoor and drive-in movie theaters, but I rarely attended any of them until my last two years of high school.

* * *

One of the most popular games in grade school was softball, and that was replaced by baseball in high school. Baseball is sometimes called "America's national pastime." For 75 years from the late 19th century until around 1950, the name was entirely appropriate. Not only did professional baseball, at both the minor and major league levels, prosper during this period, but thousands of companies, businesses and small towns all over America sponsored baseball teams composed of local players who competed in amateur leagues and tournaments. Professional baseball stars like Ty Cobb, Babe Ruth, Joe DiMaggio, and Ted Williams were lionized for their extraordinary athletic abilities and accomplishments, if not always for their personal behavior.

While segregated from white baseball from the early 1890s until Jackie Robinson in 1947, African American men had their own rich tradition of participation in amateur and professional baseball. Men dominated the baseball world, but there were also professional and amateur baseball and its close cousin, fast-pitch softball, teams for women. Cheering on the players during this period were huge numbers of baseball fans of all ages, genders, and demographic groups.

Other sports like basketball and football were not yet as well established or popular with spectators or players as they later became. Golf and tennis were mainly for wealthy people with lots of leisure time, but baseball had universal appeal. Before the era of television, radio broadcasting of games beginning in the 1920s accelerated the growth of baseball's popularity.

With its population of less than fifty, Sharpsburg was too small to be incorporated but nevertheless it had a men's town baseball team during the early twentieth century until the late 1940s. Dad and two of his brothers, Andy and Bones, were members of the Sharpsburg Speeds in the 1920s and 1930s. According to Dad, Andy was the star second baseman who "would often go a whole season without making an error." Dad said he played third base and Bones was a pitcher, but they were not regulars in the lineup. Dad may have been overly modest about his own skills, as his brother Lee told Harry and Jerry both Andy and Dad were good players. At any rate, the Speeds had a great deal of local success against other town teams in Mercer and adjoining counties.

One year in the late 1930s the Speeds entered a tournament for town baseball teams and won several games advancing to the final round in Kansas City before being eliminated. Dad said several carloads of fans from Sharpsburg and nearby farms made the 15-hour drive to watch their local team compete in the big city. Until the late 1940s, the Speeds played each Sunday afternoon in the summer with their home games at the Sharpsburg school baseball field.

Dad no longer played, but he and the whole family enjoyed attending the games. Mom packed a picnic basket with food. During the game, we socialized with our friends and neighbors. The younger kids had lots of fun with their friends tracking down foul balls that frequently landed in the field behind home plate and across the road from the ball field.

The nearest major league baseball team was in Cincinnati,

about 100 miles south of our farm. Prior to the 1953 season the Cincinnati baseball team changed their name from Reds to Redlegs in response to the fervent anti-communism in the country. Communists were referred to as "reds," and the team wanted to avoid anything that smacked of communism. Cincinnati baseball fans never reacted well to the name change; in fact, most continued to call their team the Reds, its nickname since 1890.

Finally, following the 1958 season, Reds management decided anti-"Redleg" sentiment among fans outweighed any remaining pressure from anti-communists and the Redlegs officially became the Reds again. Dad was a life-long fan of the Cincinnati Reds. When the farm work schedule permitted, he listened to radio broadcasts of Reds games. In retirement, he rarely missed watching games that were televised or listening on the radio to ones that were not. He loved to sit on the porch in his wooden rocker with the radio beside him tuned to a Reds' game.

When Jim and I were in middle school and high school, we sometimes listened to Reds games, too. Our rural location meant our reception of WLW, the Cincinnati station that belonged to Reds owner Powell Crosley, was not always clear. When the Reds played the Cubs, we often listened to Chicago's WLS which had a strong signal instead of battling the static on the Reds station. The WLS broadcast was clear, but the downside was we had to put up with Bert Wilson, the Cubs' announcer who was a wildly enthusiastic Cub fan. During those broadcasts, we spent most of our time grumbling about Wilson's bias and making fun of him when the Cubs disappointed him as they often did in those years.

The most exciting Reds vs Cubs game I remember was one we listened to on WLS. It was played in Cincinnati, and the Cubs were ahead 3-1 with two outs in the bottom of the ninth inning. Assuming the Cubs would win, Bert Wilson was already in the midst of his end-of-victory gloating. He quieted a little when two

Reds reached base, and Wally Post came to bat. Wilson was completely crushed and nearly speechless when Wally hit a three-run home run to win the game, while Jim and I ran exuberantly around the yard laughing and yelling in celebration!

Wally Post, a Mercer Countian who played right field for the Cincinnati Reds in the mid-fifties, was one of our favorite sports heroes. Wally grew up on a farm near St. Wendelin, a few miles from our farm, and Dad knew Frank Post, Wally's father. My first trip of more than 25 or 30 miles from home was in the summer of 1953 or 1954 to attend a Reds game in which Wally was the honored player.

1957 Topps card

In the days before professional and college sports came to be dominated by the television market, sports teams did their best to maximize their main source of income, home game attendance. An important part of that effort was to recruit the best amateur players from the team's region of the country on the theory more regional players translated into more interest in the team from people who lived close enough to attend some games each year. As a further attendance building strategy, team management specified a game each year in honor of each regional player. My debut at a live major league baseball game was, appropriately, on Wally Post Night at the Reds' Crosley Field.

My memories of that special night are still vivid. Dad, Jim and I joined Uncle Lee, Harry and Jerry in Lee's car for the 200-mile roundtrip. It is the only time I ever went to such an event with my Dad, although later some high school friends, often including Harry and Jerry, and I drove to several Reds games each summer. Before the game, Wally Post was introduced and presented with several gifts from Reds supporters.

The Reds had a great game against the visiting Chicago Cubs. Reds right-hander Art Fowler pitched a complete game beating the Cubs' Warren Hacker 8-1. Ted Kluszewski, Reds slugging first baseman, hit two homeruns into the right-field bleachers. The Reds' popular radio broadcaster in the 1950s, Waite Hoyt, a former Yankee pitcher and teammate of Babe Ruth and Lou Gehrig in the 1920s, named those bleachers the "Burgerville" in honor of the Reds' radio sponsor, Burger Beer. Wally Post had one single in four times at bat. After the game, Lee and Dad decided to drive across a bridge over the Ohio River before heading home so we could say we had been in Kentucky. It was the first time for all six of us.

Around the time of our Wally Post Night trip, we began to lose interest in collecting baseball cards. Jim and I became interested in magazines about baseball and other sports. We subscribed to *Sport* magazine for many years beginning in 1952, and we played more baseball and softball ourselves. The four of us often paired up–Jerry and Jim, Harry and me–playing catch and calling balls and strikes over a home plate.

We all four played on the elementary school softball team when we were eligible in grades six through eight. Pick-up games that included our sisters and other neighbors, in particular, the Sutter, Schmitz, and Wendel families who lived nearby, were also fun for all of us.

Jim and I began to compete in sponge rubber baseball games when I was in sixth or seventh grade. To help us, Dad built a portable wooden backstop that was perhaps 6 feet wide and 8 feet high. The batter stood in front of the backstop placed 60 feet from the pitcher who stood at the huge front of the barn. We made up rules about what was an out and what was a single, double, triple, and homerun depending on where the batted ball hit the barn. Then we played games according to baseball rules, registering runs, hits, strikeouts and walks just as in a real baseball game.

To add to our fantasy, we pretended to be some of our favorite major leaguers. When I was pitching, I was usually Robin Roberts, Phillies right-handed ace in the 1950s and presently in the Baseball Hall of Fame. Jim was often Bobby Schantz, a left-hander like Jim, who in 1952 won 24 games for a seventh-place Philadelphia Athletics team and was named Most Valuable Player in the American League.

Although we were both natural right-handed batters, we batted left-handed or right-handed to match the major leaguer we were pretending to be. For a short time, we decided we should both be able to pitch with either hand, so we switched gloves and I threw left-handed and Jim right-handed with awkward results. After a day or two of this experiment, we gave it up because our previously unused throwing arms were terribly sore. As we got older, we used a real baseball rather than a rubber one and hit out to an open field instead of at the front of the barn, but we continued to play variations of this two-person game through my years in high school.

For three summers beginning after my eighth-grade year, Dad allowed us to make our own baseball field. We mowed the grass, dragged the infield, and laid out the bases and pitcher's mound. On Sunday afternoons, at least 10 or 15 Sharpsburg kids came over and played on our diamond. That was great, but one Sunday we got the idea to invite some guys our age in Burkettsville to bike the three miles to our diamond and play against us.

They agreed and we played them several times, sometimes on our diamond and sometimes on the Burkettsville school diamond. It was good competitive fun, and the recruiting and scheduling we did was a valuable learning experience. Dad's only role was to allow us to use his farmland for a baseball field. Everything else was our project.

As a way to involve our younger brothers and sisters in playing softball in our barnyard, Jim and I invented rules for a game we called "Get the Dumps Out." Our younger siblings were on a single team playing against the two of us, but they were always at bat. Jim and I alternated between pitching and playing in the field. Together we did our best to cover the entire field, which was not large. I suppose the bases were about 40 feet apart.

One rule in our favor was "pitcher's hand was out," that is, if the pitcher got the ball before the batter reached first base the batter was out. Our goal was to keep "the dumps" from scoring any runs before they made three outs, and repeat that inning after inning. That worked pretty well for a few years until some of the younger kids like Doris and Rick became too good with the bat. Jim and I finally grew tired of running all over the barnyard chasing their well-placed hits, and that put an end to "Getting the Dumps Out."

* * *

I liked to play baseball, but I was also a nerd about the statistical aspects of the game. I knew the all-time records and record holders in most statistical categories both for a single season and lifetime. I loved to pore over the season-by-season, lifetime records of hall of famers and current superstars as well as all statistics from the current season.

From the time I was in fifth or sixth grade, Jim and I often played a board game called *All-Star Baseball*. In this game, major league all-stars of the past and present were each represented by a cardboard disk. The disk was fit over a spinner when the player "came to bat." Each numbered sector of the disk represented a batting outcome like a fly ball, single or home run. Sluggers like Babe Ruth had larger homerun sectors than singles hitters; in fact, a player's disk was designed to match his actual batting statistics. We enjoyed this game but it was limited, focusing entirely on hitting. Pitching and fielding were not accounted for in any way.

Sometime during eighth grade an ad in *Baseball Digest* caught my eye. It was a small advertisement for a fantasy game that allowed those playing to be the manager of any one of the major league baseball teams. Based on rolling two dice simultaneously, a large red one and a small white one, it was an improvement over *All-Star Baseball* since pitching and fielding were taken into account, not just hitting. The game was called *American Professional Baseball Association* or *APBA* and it appeared to fit my nerdy baseball stat interests perfectly.

The cost of *APBA* was $19.95, more money than I had at the time. This was during the time Jim and I agreed to share our money, and he was interested in the game, too. But even together we didn't have enough. What to do? Fortunately, my Solemn Communion was in early May of my eighth-grade year, and I received more than enough in gifts from my baptismal sponsors, Aunt Lizzie and Uncle Lee, and my grandparents to order *APBA* through the mail.

Up to then, I had a dismal record of mail order purchases from comic book or sports magazine advertisements. During our playing cowboys phase, I was frustrated that our cap guns often misfired when they were loaded with a roll of caps. When I saw an ad in a comic book for what sounded like a real gun that shot blanks, I sent my money. After what seemed like weeks waiting for the gun's arrival in the mail, I opened the box to find a cardboard gun with "gunpowder" that appeared to be a lot like baking soda. When I loaded the gun and fired, the sound was a muffled "thump" like hitting a pile of baking soda with a soupspoon. I was devastated.

A few years later when Jim and I were playing our two-person rubber baseball game and trying to make the ball curve, we were attracted by an ad in a sports magazine for a "trick baseball" that, in the ad, appeared to curve in unpredictable ways no matter how you threw it. Again, we sent in the required cash. The trick baseball was a hollow rubber ball, the size of a baseball, with a small, hard rubber weight attached to the inside of its cover.

Because of the off-center weight, the ball wobbled when we threw it but it didn't curve. To make matters worse, a big rip appeared in the cover the first time one of us hit our trick baseball with a bat. With these mail order fiascoes fresh in mind, I was concerned *APBA* may fall far short of expectations.

I was wrong. *APBA* was all I expected it to be and more. I was hooked. The game included cards for 400 major league players, 25 per team, designed to match their 1955 statistics. In my imagination, I felt in control of the entire major leagues. At first, Jim and I played some games against each other as managers of different teams, but soon I made up some rules about what a manager would do in given situations and began to play the games by myself.

In time, I became efficient at playing and could complete a game in ten or fifteen minutes. When I had time to play, I usually set up a card table in front of the television in the living room so I wouldn't miss out on any family activities. The part that was most fun for me was to keep batting and pitching records and, as the season progressed, watch them converge to the real 1955 statistics. I told Jim about all this, but he was less interested in playing the game than I was and it soon became my obsession. I played four full 8-team league seasons of 616 games per season over the next three or so years.

In retrospect, I could have made better use of my time, but there were some pluses to playing *APBA*. Besides keeping me out of trouble during my adolescent years, my *APBA* playing helped me learn to focus on a task while shutting out all background noise, a useful skill for a student, professor or writer. *APBA* play gave me a good intuition about statistical simulations and developed my interest in randomness and probability. The records I kept and statistics I computed were all with paper and pencil, so my data handling skills also improved. In my first semester at UD, I typed all my *APBA* records as practice for the typing class I was required to take.

Having spent so many hours with the 1955 major league baseball statistics, for years I had a phenomenal memory of them. I later learned some of the statistical geeks who influenced major league baseball teams to make much more, and more creative, use of statistics by the 1990s had begun by playing *APBA*. The 2003 book and 2011 Brad Pitt movie, *Money Ball*, describes an example of this relatively new statistical emphasis in major league baseball.

I enjoyed the *APBA* game for a long time, but I completely lost interest by the end of high school. A year or two later, I put an ad in *Baseball Digest* and sold the game along with the typed records of my four seasons of play for $40, double our original investment. I was satisfied with the sale, but sometime later I got a long letter from my game's new owner, who thanked me profusely for the game and records. He thought he had gotten a good deal, and he went on and on praising the records I had kept. He didn't know how I could have given them up, but he assured me he appreciated them and would take good care of them. Perhaps I should have listed the game and records at a higher price.

Interestingly, basketball, the sport that would be my ticket to a college education, did not become a major focus for me until high school. In elementary school or as we usually called it, grade school, I had other interests.

4 GRADE SCHOOL

Roman Catholicism as experienced in St. Paul's Catholic Church in Sharpsburg largely provided the basis for the ethics and morality in our family life. My siblings and I were baptized as Catholics within a week or so of birth, made our first confession and received first communion in second grade, and were confirmed sometime after second grade but before eighth grade by the Archbishop of Cincinnati.

While attending Sharpsburg Elementary School, we went to mass Monday through Friday, to confession bi-weekly and attended classes in the Baltimore Catechism and Bible History taught by the priest. Mom, Dad, and all their children of at least school age attended mass every Sunday and every Holy Day of Obligation. The family also attended many of the evening church services during special times in the church like Lent, Advent, and Holy Week (the week before Easter).

Families did not sit together in church. The children sat in the front three or four rows of pews, girls on the left and boys on the right, and the adults in the pews behind them. All females were expected to wear something on their head, a scarf or hat of some sort. Until the church made changes in the early 1960s, priests in all Catholic parishes celebrated most of the mass and other

St. Paul's Catholic Church, Sharpsburg

church services in Latin with their backs to their parishioners.

All our grade school classmates and their families were St. Paul's members who kept the same schedule of religious activities as we did, so the church had a social as well as religious function in the community. In fact, the church was an integral part of the community in many ways. St. Paul's parishioners were nearly all farmers or members of farm families. Farms in the area were no more than two or three hundred acres and usually less, and the success of a farmer's crops on such small farms was heavily dependent on the weather at crucial times during the growing season.

In support of the farmers, St. Paul's and other Catholic churches in the area offered special services and prayers for good weather each spring and summer. Pat reminded me when a dangerous storm was in progress, Mom lit a blessed candle or burned palms we had gotten in church on Palm Sunday, and we prayed the rosary.

The parish priest was an important member of the community, who was sometimes included in family decisions now considered to be the responsibility of parents. For example, when my older sisters got their first full-time jobs, Mom and Dad asked the parish priest how much of my sisters' wages should be contributed to the family budget. When they were teenagers living at home, their parents kept nearly all the money they earned. With the priest's wise counsel, they decided to charge my sisters a fair rent for their room and board but let them keep most of their wages. I remember briefly thinking I should become a priest so people would value my advice and never criticize me.

Catholicism as we experienced it had many fairly precise behavioral rules whose violation was considered a minor (venial) or serious (mortal) sin. The belief was if you died with sins on your soul, you went to purgatory or hell rather than directly to heaven but your sins were forgiven if you confessed them to a priest in the sacrament of confession. Mom and Dad were not averse to using fear of sin in their child-rearing techniques, but in my early memories parental threats that "Santa will not bring you anything" were more common and far more effective than the "sin card". The possibility of no presents next Christmas was scarier to me than the vague threat of hell-fire and damnation at some time in the far distant future.

Christmas time for me was a magical time of year. Getting a few toys and some candy on Christmas Eve was nice, but I enjoyed the weeks and days leading up to Christmas even more. The anticipation of Christmas was reinforced everywhere in our environment: the beautiful Christmas trees and crib scene in church, the Christmas carols in

Dave takes stock of his Christmas toys.

75

school, on the radio and in church, our school Christmas party, picking out and decorating our Christmas tree, the Christmas editions of mail-order catalogues, the special Christmas shows on many of our favorite radio programs, movies and comic books with Christmas themes, and the weather getting colder adding to the anticipation of a white Christmas.

I believed unquestioningly in Santa Claus until I found some toys hidden in the hog pen a few days before Christmas one year. I think I was in fourth grade. If my parents or older sisters had told me Santa's elves left them there so Santa's sleigh wasn't too full on Christmas Eve, I would have believed it. Instead they took the opportunity to tell me there was no Santa, and much of the Christmas magic was gone forever. The main fun of Christmas Eve for me after that was watching the wide-eyed excitement of my younger brothers and sisters.

A family Easter tradition was a lamb cake.

Before church reforms in the 1960s, abstaining from meat on Friday was a tradition we took seriously. When I was in high school, I sometimes went with friends to a restaurant in Fort Recovery on Friday night after a movie or a basketball game. Catholics in the group first ordered a coke and chips or some non-meat snack then, at around 11:45 p.m., ordered a hamburger timed to arrive at midnight. If it arrived a few minutes early, we waited patiently watching the clock hands and diving into the burger at precisely midnight. My friends who were not Catholic just laughed at this strange behavior.

The sins emphasized most by the church had to do with sex.

Unmarried teenagers and young adults were taught many taboos aimed at prohibiting all sexual activity before marriage. After marriage, natural family planning was the sanctioned method of birth control.

As hard as the Catholic Church came down on matters of sex, there was little restriction on drinking alcohol, dancing, and playing cards including gambling. In fact, these three activities were the main sources of entertainment for many teenagers and young adults in Mercer County. Drinking to excess, in particular, sometimes had tragic consequences with many deaths and injuries caused by drunken driving, including the deaths in car accidents of three of my grade school classmates before the age of twenty.

Overall, the church supported the family and community in providing me with strong feelings of security, as well as humility and obedience. I tried to behave in line with church rules, more for the approval of the significant adults in my life than

Linda's first and Pat's solemn communion (8th grade) with surviving grandparents

from religious conviction. I have fond memories of my Holy Communion, Confirmation, and Solemn Communion. At each event, my grandparents and Uncle Lee and Aunt Lizzie, my baptismal sponsors, and their families were invited to the church ceremony and then to our house for a meal and socializing to celebrate the occasion. The attention and gifts of money, though small amounts by today's standards, were special to me and rare in my hardscrabble childhood.

* * *

I served as an altar boy from fifth through eighth grades. Altar boys, usually two at each mass, were expected to give the response in Latin to the priest's Latin prayers. Middle school boys who did not speak, read, or understand the language could hardly be expected to excel at this task, and my peers and I lived up to the low expectation. Mainly, we mumbled incoherently through brief responses like "Et cum spiritu tuo" in response to the priest's "Dominus vobiscum." Longer prayers like the Confiteor, began with a loud clear "Confiteor Deo omnipotenti" followed by several seconds of mumbling, a loud and clear "mea culpa, mea culpa, mea maxima culpa", more mumbling, and finally a clear "Amen."

My attitude toward being an altar boy was mixed. By eighth grade, I was several inches taller than the priest, and I felt embarrassed when I overheard a remark about my height from a parishioner. Some of the longer services were physically challenging for an altar boy, such as the Good Friday devotion service from noon until 3:00 p.m. that required extended periods of kneeling.

On the positive side, each altar boy was asked to serve daily mass for one week sometime during the summer. I liked that week best, starting with the 1.5-mile bike ride at 7:00 a.m. when the heat of the summer day had not yet set in. The mass was short with only a few people in attendance usually including Grandma Schoen who sometimes invited me to her house for milk and cookies before I biked home. Both priests I served mass for were respectful and kind to their altar boys, and they were especially relaxed at the summer weekday masses.

St. Charles Seminary Main Building

The best thing for me about being a St. Paul's altar boy in those days was the annual summer Server's Picnic for all altar boys in Mercer County sponsored by the seminarians at St. Charles' Seminary near Carthagena. The Seminary prepared priests for the Precious Blood order. The seminarians were mostly young men in their early twenties, and they knew how to produce a day chockfull of fun activities for middle school boys. The all-day servers' picnic was held on the spacious seminary grounds. The day began with mass in the seminary chapel. The chapel's beauty was breathtaking, and the Gregorian chant of the seminarians was a welcome break from the off-key choir at St. Paul's.

Immediately after mass, we rushed out to the open recreation area to the south of the main building where our hosts had assembled game and food stands similar to those at a carnival.

They charged us a dime for a hot dog and a nickel for a soft drink. The pond was available for wading and swimming, and we could wait in line for a ride on the small pontoon. The straw bale tunnel the seminarians built for us was like those we built in our barn, except more cleverly constructed. I rushed through it from beginning to end, then ran immediately back to the beginning to get in line to do it again and again.

In the afternoon, each parish entered a softball team in the Server's Picnic tournament. Most years St. Paul's team was competitive, winning a three-inning game or two, but the larger parishes, Coldwater or St. Henry, usually won the championship. My last server's picnic, in the summer after eighth grade, was special. Not only did our team finish second in the tournament, our best finish ever, but also the seminarians surprised us with an appearance by Wally Post, right fielder for the Cincinnati Reds.

In the middle of the 1955 baseball season, the best of his career (.309 with 40 homeruns and 109 runs batted in), Wally was at home in St. Henry for the National versus American League All-Star Game break. He said a few words reminiscing fondly about his own years at the Server's Picnic. He also joked he was not in the All-Star game that year but his shoes were. Wally's teammate, All-Star center fielder Gus Bell, had borrowed a pair of spiked baseball shoes from him for the game.

After Wally's talk, the altar boys lined up to meet him and get his autograph. For me, it was a memorable ending to four years of Server's Picnics. I still feel grateful to those generous seminarians for producing such enjoyable days. Tragically, a year or two after I last attended a boy drowned in the pond at the Server's Picnic, and the tradition was interrupted for a few years.

* * *

Adjacent to St. Paul's Catholic Church in Sharpsburg was the red brick elementary schoolhouse. Originally it had just one room, but the building had been expanded to four classrooms by the time I attended grades one through eight there. At the time, there was no kindergarten available in the area. Arthur H. Rose was the head teacher and later principal at Sharpsburg Elementary School from sometime in the 1930s to 1960 when he was promoted to Superintendent of the Southwest School District in Fort Recovery. He was a Catholic native of Mercer County, born in St. Sebastian about ten miles away.

Sharpsburg Elementary School in early 1960s

In addition to being teacher and principal, Teacher Rose served as the parish organ player, choir leader, bell ringer, groundskeeper, and maintenance man. He, his wife, and two children lived in a parish-owned house directly across the road from the school building. Over the years, parishioners sometimes privately complained about the financial deal he received on the house, although no one knew exactly what it was. At any rate, by the time I attended grade school Teacher Rose was unquestionably a pillar of the community.

Sharpsburg Elementary School was a public school, but all the teachers were Catholic and all the students were from Catholic families. In most ways, the school operated like a Catholic school affiliated with St. Paul's Church. After arriving on the public school buses in the morning, all students attended mass at St. Paul's. During the regular school day, the parish priest came over to school to teach religion classes, and students were scheduled by grade to go to Confession in the church.

First Communion and Confirmation preparations were handled like classes in the regular school curriculum. School was not scheduled on Catholic Holy Days, and students attended extra church services during Lent, Advent, and Holy Week. No one objected to this mode of operation until long after I finished eighth grade. In the early 1960s, some protestants in Fort Recovery filed a lawsuit against the school district that put an end to daily mass, religious instruction in the school building, and church services during school time.

In my years at Sharpsburg Elementary, it was a pretty basic 4R school, that is, reading, 'riting, 'rithmetic, and religion. With the exception of religion classes taught by the parish priest there were no special classes or teachers for music, art, or anything else, although in our regular classrooms we occasionally sang patriotic or nostalgic songs like "America the Beautiful," "My Country 'tis of Thee," "The Olde Oaken Bucket," "My Old Kentucky Home", "Home on the Range." "I've Been Working on the Railroad," "You are My Sunshine," "My Bonny Lies Over the Ocean." and "Way Down Upon the Suwanee River."

Teacher Rose was the choir director at St. Paul's, and he directed the seventh and eighth grade in the presentation of a musical program for parents each year. But it was wrong to say we were taught anything about music. For example, I could never carry a tune. Rather than teach me to sing or at least encourage me to try, when my class began to sing a song Teacher Rose rushed to tap me on the shoulder as a signal I should just mouth the words.

One Friday afternoon each month, the entire student body assembled in the auditorium that doubled as the seventh and eighth grade classroom to watch a movie. The school had no gymnasium. I think the movies, which were fairly recent releases of feature films, were provided by the Ohio Department of Education to give students in rural areas enrichment experiences. As a movie fan, I loved all of them. Even Teacher Rose thought some of them were so good he scheduled and advertised in the weekly parish bulletin a nighttime showing free of charge for any adults in St. Paul's who were interested. Walt Disney's *Pinocchio* and *Cinderella* and Judy Garland in *Meet Me in St. Louis* are three films I remember he showed at night.

I entered first grade in fall of 1947. Mrs. Blanche Vonderhaar, my first and second grade teacher, was a nice lady, and I found school to be pretty easy, though often boring. My favorite time of day was recess. It was great to let off steam, running and playing on the playground. Besides playing on the playground equipment like the slides and swings, we played many versions of tag, hide and seek, red rover, crack the whip and my personal favorite at the time, softball. I was slim and either the tallest or second tallest in my class throughout my school years. My height coupled with pretty good natural athletic ability meant I was among the first chosen for most games.

My performance in the classroom was always good, although I was not as conscientious as some of my female classmates. I was punctual with assignments, but not always neat and tidy. Math was my favorite subject from a young age. Numbers and pattern recognition did not confuse me as they did some of my classmates, but my verbal skills were just a little above the national average.

On standardized tests like the *Iowa Test of Basic Skills* (ITBS), my national percentile in verbal tests was usually in the 60s while it was in the 90s on other subtests and in the high 90s in mathematics. At the time, I did not think much about those differences in achievement levels. Much later, in the mid-1970s, when H.D. Hoover, the main mathematics author of the ITBS, and I became good friends, we agreed growing up among people of few words may have hindered the development of my verbal abilities, but farm experiences and love of sports statistics helped some aspects of my mathematical ability. At any rate, I was comfortable with mathematical content but sometimes felt intimidated in situations where verbal skills were crucial.

In spite of these verbal limitations, I was at or near the top of my class of 14 in grade school in all subjects including reading and spelling. Once in second grade I remember getting some special attention for a writing assignment. Mrs. Vonderhaar had us write a short story about anything that was of interest to us. At the time, my fantasy life was mainly populated with cowboy heroes like the Lone Ranger, Roy Rogers, Gene Autry, and Hopalong Cassidy. At every opportunity, I read their comic books and big little books, listened to their radio shows, and watched their movies.

Big little books were thick and hard covered, but about half the height and width of a typical book.

When charged with writing about a topic "of interest to me," I wrote a story about the Lone Ranger with a plot similar to what may have appeared in a cowboy comic book at the time. I don't remember the details, but I ended the story with a shoot-out in which Tonto and the Lone Ranger decimated the bad guys. To describe the shoot-out, I included every noise used in comic books for gunshots or fist fights I could think of like bang, blam, kerblam, ping, blast, biff, pow, and so on.

The day after I turned in my story I saw Mrs. Vonderhaar show it to Teacher Rose. I couldn't hear their whispered comments so I have never been sure whether they were impressed that a second grader was so creative or were shocked at the level of violence in my story or something else. I got a good grade on the story but no other feedback I can remember.

My aunt, Mrs. Cecilia Schoen, the wife of Dad's oldest brother, Bones, was my teacher for two years in the room shared by third and fourth graders. I liked Sis, as the family called her, and she took a special interest in my siblings and me when we were in her classes. By fourth grade, I was finding little challenge from my school subjects, but I was beginning to enjoy reading a variety of books.

Sis as Dave's (in front of the Christmas tree) second grade teacher in 1963-64.

In addition to books that featured current cowboy heroes, I enjoyed stories about The Hardy Boys, Bobbsey Twins, and, influenced by my sisters, Trixie Belden and Ginny Gordon. At the Fort Recovery Public Library, I discovered Tarzan, Zane Grey, H. G. Wells, and children's biographies of famous pioneers, inventors, politicians and athletes. About then or a little later, I also began to read every book about the history of baseball in the town library.

In her two-grade room, Sis typically gave students in one grade an assignment to keep them busy while she taught a lesson to those in the other grade. Knowing some students were able to complete her assignments quickly and easily, Sis allowed us to read our own books between our lessons as long as we were quiet.

One day when I was in fourth grade, I became so engrossed in the book I was reading I didn't notice Sis had finished her third-grade lesson, and the students were filing out to attend a church service next door. The other students got a big laugh at my surprise and embarrassment when I finally broke the spell of my book and realized I was the only student left seated in the room. Evidently, Sis was amused too as she couldn't resist frequently telling that story about me at family events even when I was in my thirties.

My fourth-grade year was also memorable for the 1950 Thanksgiving weekend blizzard, often referred to as Ohio's most severe winter storm of the twentieth century. On the afternoon of Thanksgiving, the temperature was in the forties or fifties and there was no precipitation. The sky was dark and getting darker, eventually becoming the deepest steely gray I ever remember.

The temperature was dropping rapidly, and sometime around six or seven p.m. light snow began to fall accompanied by 40 or 50 mile per hour winds. The temperature dropped to around zero, the snow and winds continued through the night, all the next day and the day after with only occasional letting up. We had at least two feet of snow with drifts of eight or ten feet.

A few years ago, my cousin Larry Heitkamp reminded me his hero, Roy Rogers, and wonder horse Trigger were stranded for the weekend in Lima about 50 miles northeast of us. They were trying to reach nearby Troy for a Sunday show at Hobart Arena that, of course, had to be cancelled. The storm was even worse in eastern Ohio where in some areas three feet of snow fell with drifts up to 25 feet.

During the three or four days of the storm, we mainly stayed in the house as the snow and wind made it a struggle to make the necessary trips from the house to the barn to do the morning and evening milking and feeding. All the roads in the area were impassable due to snowdrifts until county road crews began to plow them after the snow stopped late on Sunday. The still strong winds and low temperatures made this a frustrating job, however, as substantial amounts of snow were soon blown back onto the plowed roads.

School was canceled for the full week after Thanksgiving, and I believe for some of the following week. On Wednesday or Thursday after Thanksgiving, groceries were getting low and the temperature and winds had moderated somewhat, so Dad dressed up as warmly as he could, put on his high-top winter boots, and walked across the fields to Sharpsburg pulling our sled behind him. He brought back enough groceries for another week. Most of us kids were glad for a reason not to have to go to school, but the effects of this storm lasted so long we were happy to get back.

Fifth grade was a terrible year. My teacher was a young woman in her first year of teaching, a career for which she was not well suited. Miss Smith (not her real name) was inconsistent and prone to angry outbursts with little provocation. She had clear student favorites, mostly the more outgoing and personable girls. Miss Smith did not seem to like any of the boys, and she vented her anger on any boy she caught breaking her rules of conduct. I was well behaved for the most part so I did not often suffer her wrath, but one day she caught two other boys and me violating one of her rules when she stepped out of the classroom for a few minutes. We were whispering and giggling and maybe one or more of us was out of our seat when Miss Smith abruptly re-entered the room.

She was furious, herding the three of us into the hall where she read us the riot act at some length. She then slapped each of my collaborators in crime sharply across the face. As I braced for my slap, she hissed at me through clenched teeth, "You can thank your lucky stars you wear glasses." Having just begun wearing glasses the previous summer, I did feel lucky to escape her humiliating slap although her angry and abusive words alone were more hurtful than our breach in behavior warranted.

Worse yet, at the end of the school year, Miss Smith failed both boys she slapped, causing them to repeat fifth grade. I don't know any details about their work in her class, but they were not dummies. In fact, one of them, after quitting high school at age 16, became a fighter pilot and went on to earn a Master's Degree while serving in the military. It was with great relief that Sharpsburg fifth and sixth graders greeted the news the following summer; Miss Smith was not returning in the fall.

A more experienced teacher, Mrs. Schulte, took over the fifth and sixth grade classroom that fall of my sixth-grade year. She did a much better job in the classroom than Miss Smith. She lived in Celina, the Mercer County seat, and commuted 22 miles to Sharpsburg each day. I liked her pretty well, as did most of my classmates.

Like my Aunt Sis, during the time she was teaching students in one grade, she allowed those in the other grade to read things of interest to them after finishing their assigned school work. That year I discovered the Greek and Roman myths in a reference series Mrs. Schulte had on a shelf in our classroom. They were abridged translations of the original stories, but I became fascinated with the characters and their adventures. This reading provided me some vague familiarity with and a continuing interest in classical western literature that served me well in my later studies.

A few times during sixth grade Mrs. Schulte got angry and showed her disdain for her country bumpkin students. To her, we were evidently lacking in sophistication and personal hygiene, and our countrified ways were below her standards. For the first time, I remember thinking perhaps I should feel ashamed of my family and friends, or at least of the circumstances in which we lived. Mrs. Schulte resigned at the end of the school year.

In sixth grade for the first time, I was eligible to play on the Sharpsburg Elementary boys' fast-pitch softball team that competed against other grade schools of comparable size in Mercer County. On most Friday afternoons in September and October, Sharpsburg either hosted a visiting team or traveled to one of the other schools. The girls' teams competed first, then the boys' teams. All students and teachers of grades six through eight from the competing schools attended the games and rooted for their teams.

My sixth-grade softball team; I am on the left in the first row. Classmate Fred Schmitz is first row on right and his 8th grade brother Ronnie is behind him.

This was my first experience in organized sports competition with an adult coach and organizer, Teacher Rose, and cheering fans. I loved it from the start. I played left field in sixth grade and, by the next year, I was one of the best players on our team. We had a fairly good boys' team, usually winning more often than we lost. The girls did even better. Schools we competed against included St. Joe, St. Peter, St. Anthony, Philothea, St. Wendelin, Burkettsville, Carthegena, Montezuma, Chickasaw, Fort Recovery St. Mary's, and Washington Township.

At Washington Township one Friday afternoon, I had a bad scare. I think it was during my sixth-grade year, but it may have been seventh or eighth; I'm not sure. Most of the schools we competed against were, like Sharpsburg, in a small crossroads of a town, but Washington was completely rural. The school building was on the east side of a little used north-south county road, and the ball diamond was on the west side. There were no businesses nearby and no house within a quarter mile of the school. Grain fields abutted and surrounded the school property.

As always on game days, I was full of excited anticipation of the upcoming game. Watching our girls' team cream the opposition in the company of my teammates just added to my excitement. Sometime during the girls' game, I needed to use the restroom located in the school building. I waited until the end of an inning and then, in an effort to miss as little of the game as possible, I dashed head down across the road toward the school. In all the excitement, I ran onto the road without looking in either direction, until I heard a horn honk, brakes squeal and saw the huge front end of a feed mill truck bearing down on me. I kept running as fast as I could and, in my memory at least, I barely missed being hit by the truck.

I don't think anyone but the truck driver saw this happen, and he drove on no doubt with great relief. I was a little shaken at the time, and I carefully looked both ways when I went back to the ball diamond. We beat Washington Township's team handily that afternoon although I don't remember any details of the game. I didn't tell anyone except Jim about my close call for a long time. When I happen to think about that big truck coming toward me, I realize how lucky I was that day so long ago.

The same year my fourth-grade sister Pat was not so lucky. The family was visiting our Aunt Lizzie who lived on a farm on the western edge of Coldwater. Pat and a group of her elementary school-aged siblings and first cousins including me decided to go play at the near-by Coldwater Park. To get there we ran across a field to a fence that separated us from the park. The gate in the fence was closed so we decided to climb over it. Pat went first, but to everyone's surprise the gate was just leaning against the end posts. It was not fastened on either end, and it fell with Pat on top of it. Her left arm was caught under the gate and was obviously broken.

Coldwater Mercy Hospital was adjacent to the park and less

than a half mile from Lizzie's farm, so the adults took her to the emergency room where a doctor set the two broken bones and put her arm in a cast. Pat remembers she was kept overnight in the hospital for observation, and the doctor told her if the bones did not stay in place he would have to put in a pin. Fortunately, no pin was needed, but left-handed Pat had the inconvenience of having to write with her right hand in school for a couple of months. Amazingly, Pat's arm was the only broken bone in the family during our childhoods.

When I was in grades seven and eight, Teacher Rose was the teacher as he had been for about twenty years. He was a no-nonsense person who achieved a strict classroom discipline by the force of his stern demeanor and the respect and fear he had earned from the students of Sharpsburg over the years. His control of the behavior of the grade school students went beyond school.

Anyone who was a Sharpsburg Elementary student in the forties and fifties vividly remembers Teacher Rose's unbelievably loud finger snap, which was the signal for the line of students who had just entered or were just leaving a church service at St. Paul's to genuflect in unison. Woe to the student who did not follow Teacher Rose's rules, even in Sunday masses. A stern talking to from Teacher Rose was the fate of many a kid who squirmed or whispered during a Sunday mass.

One of Teacher Rose's parish jobs was to ring the St. Paul Church bells every day at 6:00 a.m., noon, and 6:00 p.m., as was traditional in rural Catholic churches. During the school year, he assigned the noon bell ringing to an eighth-grade boy who he paid a small wage, 50 cents a week, I think. I was the designated noon ringer for our class, if not for the entire year at least for half of it. The smaller bells sometimes turned over if the ringer pulled the rope too hard. And, of course, I did just that once or twice as I was learning the "ropes" of the job. I was surprised and appreciative when Teacher Rose was patient with me on those occasions, as I was expecting him to be angry or at least annoyed.

Teacher Rose was stricter about in-class behavior than most of my earlier teachers, so I had no opportunity to engage in my own interests during school hours. I think he was an effective, dedicated teacher, but I felt intimidated by him. He enjoyed talking to some of the seventh and eighth grade boys, usually about farming or sports, and he liked the talkative outgoing boys better than the quiet ones like me.

One topic of Teacher Rose's conversations with his students that had great interest for me was the University of Dayton Flyers basketball team, a national power in those years. We listened to their games on radio and watched televised games at our Uncle Lee's house whenever we could. Local interest in the Flyers' exploits was high, because Bob Fiely, who had starred at Fort Recovery High School in the early fifties, was first substitute for the 1953-54 Flyers and a starter in 1954-55. Bob had been a high school classmate and friend of Teacher Rose's son, Tom, who were both in my sister Kate's class.

When I was in seventh grade, Teacher Rose, sparked by his interest in Flyer basketball and aided by the expertise and farm equipment of the fathers of two eighth-grade boys, erected a wooden pole with a basketball backboard and hoop on the school playground. Although the hoop was a few inches too high and slanted a little to the left and the playing surface was loose gravel so dribbling was unpredictable, this hoop gave me my first chance to regularly participate with my schoolmates in playground basketball.

* * *

My grade school experience laid the foundation for my future in a number of ways. I loved sports competition, at least softball and basketball, and I was among the best athletes in my peer group. My size was a contributing factor as I was about six feet tall at the end of eighth grade but still very slim. More importantly, I had a quietly growing confidence I was one of the best students among my classmates, especially in mathematics. My confidence in my academic abilities was enhanced by the fact many of my siblings were also among the top students in their classes.

Growing confidence or not, when Tony Homan, a farmer neighbor, asked me during the winter of my eighth or ninth grade year what I wanted to be when I got out of school, I couldn't think of anything but a farmer or working at the New Idea. I told him I'd probably be a farmer. He seemed a little disappointed to hear me say that, but he assured me, "Farming is a noble profession."

In truth, I had given little thought to my future, preferring to think school would never end. When I mulled over the question later that day, I couldn't see myself as a farmer but except for factory work I had no other models. I had never considered the possibility of attending college and had only a vague idea of career options open to me if I did attend. I remember thinking I would most likely work at the New Idea, but I was only 13 or 14 and the thought soon passed as my mind was completely dominated by high school. Thinking about what came after would have to wait.

5 INTO HIGH SCHOOL

Like many men in rural areas in his generation, my Grandpa Schoen was critical of people who wasted their time on books and school when there was farm work to be done. He often made fun of my siblings and me if he saw us reading a book, calling us "bookworms". Before the practice violated truancy laws, he made sure his sons quit going to school each spring when the weather allowed the work in the fields to begin. To him going to school was a waste of time, and everyone should quit as soon as possible.

He was adamant about girls in this regard, since in his outspoken view they were going to get married, raise kids, and do house work anyway. They may as well start as soon as they could. Mom and Dad were not as dubious about the value of education as Grandpa but, like American society of the 1940s and 1950s, they were less supportive of education for their daughters than for their sons.

I was fortunate to have siblings who helped pave the way for me in high school, but my oldest sister Kate had a hard time. Our farm was located in the Fort Recovery High School (FRHS) district, but in the late 1940s there was a controversy on the Fort Recovery school board about whether their school buses would pick up the Catholic students.

The board members who were raising the issue were in the minority, but this upset Dad who could be stubborn and short sighted. With little thought about the consequences, he decided his children would go to the "Catholic high school" in St. Henry. In reality, both St. Henry High School (SHHS) and FRHS were public schools, but the student body at SHHS was nearly 100 percent Catholic whereas one-third to one-half of FRHS's was not Catholic.

When Kate was ready to start high school in fall of 1948, our parents enrolled her in SHHS where she was the only student from her Sharpsburg Elementary class. She had to be driven over a mile each morning to catch the bus to SHHS, a distance she usually walked in the other direction after being dropped off in the afternoon when the weather was good. After the weather turned cold in winter of her freshman year, Kate stayed in St. Henry during the week with Grandma and Grandpa Heitkamp.

Grandpa was ill in fall of her sophomore year, so Kate stayed next door at Mom's sister Mamie's house. After Grandpa passed away that Christmas, Grandma did not like being alone so she often stayed with Mamie, which meant there was no longer a room for Kate. Although a good student, she dropped out of SHHS in January. Dad was ready to keep her out of school, but she was not yet 16. In February Kate enrolled in FRHS and completed her sophomore year, then dropped out of school legally when she turned 16 in August 1950. Years later, she earned a high school diploma by passing the GED exam.

Kate's ordeal cleared the way for all of us to attend FRHS starting with Ginny as a freshman that fall, but Mom and Dad encouraged both Ginny and Eileen to quit school when they were 16. After Ginny resisted the pressure to quit and continued on to graduate as valedictorian of her class, our parents seem to have decided graduating from high school was OK after all. They did not suggest any of their other children should quit high school.

* * *

After graduating from Sharpsburg Elementary, attending Fort Recovery High School in fall of 1955 was like moving to a new school district for me. My freshman class included students from at least five different elementary schools, and three or four of the kids who had been my classmates in elementary school went to a Darke County high school. Of the roughly 50 ninth-graders in my class, I knew only nine or ten of them.

This was also the first time I attended school with anyone who was not a Catholic living on a farm or in Sharpsburg. Most of the non-Catholics lived in the town of Fort Recovery and attended one of its several protestant churches. I don't recall any issues related to differences in religion when I was in high school. Religious differences would have been an issue for Mom and Dad and for many protestant parents at the time if I had seriously dated a girl who was not Catholic. Religiously mixed marriages were definitely frowned upon, but when I was in high school serious dating and marriage couldn't have been further from my mind.

My transition was helped a lot by my four older sisters who had gone to FRHS before me and done well. Ginny, in particular, was a perfectionist who rarely earned anything but the best test scores and grades. Teacher Rose was impressed when Ginny made the highest score of any Sharpsburg student in his memory on the Ohio Eighth Grade Test, although later one or two of my younger siblings did even better. In ninth grade Ginny scored second in the state of Ohio on a state algebra test, unprecedented for a FRHS student, and during her high school career she often earned local newspaper coverage for her outstanding accomplishments in school.

Besides Ginny being valedictorian of her class, Janice, who was a junior when I was a freshman, went on to be third in her class. Because of their accomplishments, our family became known in the local area for being talented in school. Encouraged by this reputation I assumed I'd do well in high school, and I did, regularly making the A honor roll.

Janice, Linda, Eileen, Marilyn, Jim, Rick

Our family's success in high school continued after me as all my siblings were above average students, and many were at or near the tops of their classes. Pat and Rick were valedictorians, and Jim was salutatorian. Doris and Dan also ranked near the tops of their classes.

One thing I disliked about high school was the long bus ride. Janice and I boarded the same bus at the end of our lane as our younger siblings and the Weitzel kids from across the road. There were thirteen Weitzel kids around a year to a year and a half apart in age, and the oldest was four years younger than me. By my senior year and continuing for several years after that, fifteen or more students from the two families boarded the bus at the end of our lane each morning.

The bus completed its route picking up FRHS and Sharpsburg students, then drove to Sharpsburg to drop the elementary students at school. From there, the driver had a new route picking up more FRHS students and some Fort Recovery Elementary School students as it meandered its way toward Fort Recovery. The entire trip to school took 30 to 45 minutes, about twice as long as my bus trip in earlier years.

FRHS was not a strong college preparatory high school at the time, but with few exceptions the teachers had undergraduate majors or minors in the subject matter they were teaching. Most came from rural or small town backgrounds in Mercer or nearby counties, so the students identified with them to a large extent. I liked many of my classes and appreciated having teachers with specialized subject matter knowledge. Homework expectations were regular but modest, perhaps a little greater than in elementary school.

As a freshman with no plans for college, I enrolled in Vocational Agriculture as well as Algebra, American History, English, and General Science. I had two study halls on most days that gave me enough time to get my class assignments and most of my preparation for tests done in school. My mathematics teacher for all four high school years was the principal, Harold (Doc) Knapke, who had been Ginny's mathematics teacher when she was in school.

Doc Knapke helps a student with his math.

Doc was impressed with Ginny as a student, so I felt some

extra pressure to do well in his classes. Fortunately, Doc was a good teacher and math was my forte so I cruised along at or near the top of all my math classes. Doc also was a UD graduate who had been the baseball and basketball coach at FRHS for about ten years, including the great team of 1951. He was not a teacher who "buddied up" to a student, but I always felt in his quiet way he took a special interest in me. For one thing, Doc advised me to drop Vocational Agriculture and to enroll in traditional college preparatory classes only, which I did beginning in my sophomore year.

The teacher I liked best was my class's homeroom teacher, Mr. Ernie Williams, who I also had for my history courses. At the beginning of each school day for four years, all members of my class met for a ten-minute homeroom period in Mr. Williams' classroom. This time for daily announcements and messages from the school administration could easily have been routine and boring, but Mr. Williams was such a pleasant and friendly man he made it lots of fun for us. His sunny disposition helped the class develop camaraderie and feel we were an important part of the school. Our class's special relationship with Mr. Williams lasted throughout high school and was cemented in our senior year when he was assigned to chaperone us on our class trip to Washington, DC.

* * *

When I entered high school, FRHS offered just two interscholastic sports for boys, basketball and baseball, and none for girls. There were certainly outstanding girl softball players in the county at the time as they had shown in interscholastic competition in middle school. My Uncle Andy's daughter Mary Agnes Schoen, who attended Coldwater High School, was one. Two from Sharpsburg Elementary were my classmate for twelve years, Marilyn Brunswick, and her sister Wanda, who was one year older. The best all-around girl athlete at FRHS was Susan Kolp who was the school's best shortstop of either gender, but these girls had no opportunity to compete against other schools.

Some schools in the county had football teams, and when I was a junior, Mr. Tallman, the junior high basketball coach organized a FRHS football team. Only freshmen and sophomores were eligible to play. The team lasted through three or four junior varsity games, losing them all. They finally had to disband and forfeit the remainder of their games when the number of able-bodied players sank below eleven. Jon Betz scored a touchdown, which was the FRHS career scoring record in football for many years. In Spring of my senior year, a first-year teacher who had run track in college established a boys' track team, a first for FRHS. I participated as a high jumper.

The official Mercer County League (MCL) baseball season was in April and May each year, but schools with no football team scheduled eight or ten baseball games in September with practice after school on days when there was no game. Around October 1, basketball began with practice each weekday evening after school. Boys on the basketball team who had a last period study hall, which I usually did, were excused from the study hall to go to practice early.

Basketball games were scheduled, usually on Tuesday and Friday nights starting in early November and ending with the MCL tournament in early February. FRHS baseball games rarely attracted any spectators, but basketball was a popular spectator sport for students as well as for many adults and children from in and around Fort Recovery.

I had been planning since sixth grade to try out for the baseball team. Ronny Schmitz, my classmate Fred's older brother, was a junior on the team, and he assured Fred and me we'd make the team and play regularly as freshmen. I was less sure about basketball having only played pick-up games on a dirt or gravel surface. I had been interested in basketball since my older sisters began to attend FRHS when the Indians basketball team was a powerhouse.

The 1950-51 team went further in the postseason tournaments than any previous FRHS team, winning the Mercer County League tournament, the district tournament, and advancing to the final game of the regional tournament. If they had won one more game, they would have played in Columbus in the Ohio state tournament. Like most FRHS students that year, my sisters were excited about the team. The whole family listened to radio broadcasts of the tournament games and cheered loudly for the Indians.

At about that time, Ginny talked Dad into setting up a basketball hoop near the garage. It was smaller and lower than the standard size and height, and we played with a ball that was an inch less in diameter than a regulation basketball. With that first hoop, we mostly played shooting games like horse, since the rough gravel surface didn't allow for dependable dribbling. Later when I was in eighth or ninth grade, Dad used an old sewing machine frame to mount a hoop on the outside of the barn and we also put up two hoops inside the barn, all at standard height.

Dad was fine with my playing baseball as long as I kept up with my morning and evening farm chores, but he wondered "if I'd ever be as good at basketball as those town boys." At the time, I was worried Dad may be right about my basketball skills. During the fall baseball season Coach Jerry Brown urged me to try out for basketball, and, as was my usual pattern, encouragement from a significant adult was all I needed to make my decision. I tried out for and made both the Indians baseball and basketball teams.

Having pitched to Jim and my cousins for so many years, I was interested in being a pitcher. I could only throw a middling fastball as a freshman, but I suppose my 6'1" height helped convince Coach Brown to give me a try as a pitcher. That year we had a good team, winning well over half our games. I sometimes pitched batting practice, but I don't remember ever pitching in a game.

My freshman teammate, Ed Kemper, was a much better pitcher with a good curve ball. Ed was from St. Joe, and I remembered having played against him in elementary school softball. He was also a funny guy, and I enjoyed him a lot at the time and as a good friend for the rest of our lives. Ed pitched in several games, including at least one complete game in which he only gave up one or two runs. Ed's senior brother Dick was our top pitcher, pitching a no hitter in one game. I regularly played first base where I fielded well but was not much of a hitter, although I improved a little in that category each year of high school.

In my sophomore year, our team was not as good as the previous year but my pitching had improved. Playing with Jim at home over the summer, I developed a roundhouse curve ball I could control pretty well. I used it in games against Burkettsville on our home diamond that summer. I also experimented sometimes with turning my wrist out to get the ball to go toward a right-handed hitter, although I didn't trust that pitch in games until my senior year. With my curveball and fastball, I became the team's top pitcher. Unfortunately, Ed Kemper developed a sore arm and had a disappointing sophomore year, so disappointing he decided not to play baseball in our junior and senior years.

My junior year in baseball was similar to the previous one; our team was mediocre but I was the number one pitcher and usually batted third or fourth as my hitting was respectable. Our archrivals, St. Henry, had an outstanding group of athletes in the class of 1958, one year ahead of me. In both my sophomore and junior years, they had by far the best baseball team in the county, once beating us 15-0 in a game, mercifully ended after 5 innings, in which all of our batters struck out except for a fly ball to right by Ernie Sutter. St. Henry was also strong in MCL basketball during those years, though not quite as dominant as they were in baseball.

Getting home after sports practice ended at 5:30 or 6:00 was often a challenge for me. Sometimes, especially in baseball season, I got a ride with a teammate from near Sharpsburg, but often I started out walking. Six miles was a long walk, but I usually got a ride from someone I knew within the first mile or so. Once on a cold, windy day during basketball season, I walked at least two or three miles before a driver stopped. My bare ears were frozen and pretty painful when I got home and for a few days after.

* * *

In basketball as a freshman, I started at zero in experience. I was surprised by the soreness in my leg muscles during the first week or so of basketball practice, but I welcomed the opportunity to finally play on a hardwood basketball court. The court in the FRHS gym was pretty impressive to me at the time, but it was considerably smaller than regulation size of 94 by 50 feet. I'm not sure of its exact dimensions, but it was about 30 to 35 feet wide.

As for its length, on regulation courts the offensive team must get the ball over the mid-court line within ten seconds of taking possession. FRHS's court had two "ten-second" lines parallel to the mid-court line and each almost touching one of the free-throw circles. We played on even shorter courts at one or two schools where the two ten-second lines were extensions of the free-throw lines.

FRHS's court also had small, fan-shaped backboards that had little surface below the level of the basket. The size of the court and shape of the backboards were disadvantages to us in the MCL tournament which was played at the Celina High School Fieldhouse on a regulation-sized court with large rectangular backboards, much like a typical court today.

By shooting baskets for hours on our barn hoops, I had developed a pretty accurate one-handed set shot from the corner, and I was always a good free throw shooter, thanks partly to Dad. During my freshman or sophomore year, Dad built a chute with a wooden frame and tin bottom that was about 18 feet long and a few inches wider than the diameter of a basketball. By wiring one end of the chute to the backboard right under the basket in the barn, I could shoot a free throw and, if I hit the shot, the ball rolled down the chute and back to me for another shot. I spent many, many hours practicing free throws this way. It paid off as I topped my team in free throw percentage three times – sophomore in high school, senior in high school, and senior in college.

My biggest weaknesses were ball-handling and moving without the ball. I too often allowed the ball to slip through my hands so defensive players could steal it from me. Dribbling for more than a couple of bounces was beyond me. I had no instincts either for how to get open, block opponents out on rebounds, or work with teammates to move the ball, but these skills began to slowly come together. At first, I was a substitute on the reserve team, although Coach Brown gave me quite a lot of playing time. After a few games, he promoted me to starting forward on the reserves. I don't recall scoring much on the reserve team but I was becoming more comfortable on the court.

Meanwhile, the varsity basketball team was having a disappointing year, winning just three games in all. In mid-January, Coach Brown decided to bench some of his senior starters to give younger players a chance to play. He made this decision the week before we were scheduled to play at Willshire, who was undefeated and destined the next month to win the Ohio state championship in our school size classification (B). Gary Kessler, their star 6'10" center, was averaging around 35 points a game.

I was shocked beyond belief when Coach Brown told me I'd start my first varsity game against Ohio's best small school team and guard its best player. To no one's surprise, Willshire beat us handily and Kessler scored over 30 points, but I scored 8 and got over a serious, week-long case of jitters a few minutes into the game. From that game on, I was starting forward or center on the FRHS varsity in every game until the end of my senior year. As it turned out, Dad and I had not needed to worry. I was able to play basketball with those Fort Recovery town boys.

In fall of 1956 when I was a sophomore, Coach Brown took our team to see the National Basketball Association's Fort Wayne, Indiana, Zollner Pistons play a preseason game against the Syracuse Nationals in the Celina High School Fieldhouse. Coincidentally, this was the last opportunity to see NBA basketball in Mercer County as the next fall the Pistons moved to Detroit.

I was impressed with the size and skill of the professional players. The great 6'10" Syracuse center Dolph Schayes put on a shooting exhibition during pregame warm-ups, sinking one after another high arching two-handed set shots from near midcourt. I also enjoyed watching two recent graduates of the University of Dayton I had seen on television, Jack Sallee and John Horan, who were trying out for the Pistons.

Fortunately for my basketball career, I continued to grow a couple of inches a year for the next several years, reaching my adult height of 6'7" by the beginning of college. My own mother once remarked I was too tall for anything but basketball. I assume she meant it "in a good way". I was unusually tall even in a tall family in which both grandfathers, my father, two uncles, and an aunt were all at least 6 feet. My uncle Bones Schoen was tallest of the group at around 6'4". Bones also had one of the family's more notable athletic accomplishments when, at age 46, he won the 1949 Ohio Trapshoot state title.

At the beginning of my sophomore year in high school, I was

6'3", and I started the season like a house afire. In one of the first games of the year, I scored 29 points against New Knoxville, and 25 in the next game against Coldwater.

All during my freshman year and in the summer, I had been working on a turn-around jump shot to supplement my one-handed set shot, and I was very accurate from up to about 15 feet. I also began driving the baseline frequently and was quick enough and tall enough to score often on that move.

Unfortunately, as the season progressed, my offensive production cooled off, partly because some opposing coaches began to key their defenses to stopping me. Our team was better than it had been in my freshmen year, but I think our winning percentage was only around .500, somewhere near the middle of the MCL, in both my sophomore and junior years.

In high school I was often several inches taller than anyone on the opposing team.

During both those seasons, our opponents often played a combination zone and man-to-man defense, called a "box and one," in which the opposing team's best defensive man shadowed me closely all over the court while his four teammates played a four-man zone so I was effectively double-teamed when the ball was near me. Although we played against this defense frequently, we never found a good way to attack it.

Since I was double-teamed, it was not easy for my teammates to get the ball to me and my baseline drives were entirely cut off. Our narrow court made this defense even tougher. As a result, I sometimes had high scoring games, but on other nights I only got a few shots. My average per game was around 15 or 16 points each year.

I was named to the all-MCL second team as a sophomore and again as a junior, so I was considered to be among the top ten players in the county but not among the very best. According to the *Celina Daily Standard*'s sports writer, I was not much of a college basketball prospect.

This writer was not my greatest supporter, but he deserves credit for being the first person to call me Hal. Since my first cousin, Harry Schoen, lived a mile down the road from our farm when I was growing up, my family and schoolmates always called me Harold. (When they were preschoolers, Harry and Jerry called me "Arn's Har," their baby talk for "Arnold's Harold".) In my junior year, the *Standard's* sports writer referred to me as "Hardwood Hal" in one of his reports. After that I was usually Hal in the Mercer County and Dayton newspapers, and more and more people began to call me Hal.

I don't remember much about specific games during those years, but a game at Saint Henry in junior year stands out in my mind. They were leading the league at the time, and we were third or fourth. They had beaten us earlier in the season at Fort Recovery, so a victory would be sweet for us. Fired up against our top rivals, we played well that night, and the score was close the entire game. With about 20 seconds to go, we had a five-point lead and it was our ball out of bounds.

When their coach called timeout, we could hardly keep from celebrating. We were on the verge of winning at Saint Henry! Back on the court, we passed the ball in-bounds, as I recall, and they fouled one of my teammates who missed the free throw. They rebounded and with about 8 or 10 seconds to go they scored, but we were still ahead by three points with possession of the ball. Unfortunately, one of our guards threw away a pass, so with a few seconds to go they had the ball out of bounds. Coach Brown called timeout and urged us not to foul. "If they score a field goal, we still win by one point. Challenge them but whatever you do, *don't foul!*"

Somehow in the tension of the moment one of my teammates misunderstood the instructions, thinking we were supposed to foul them immediately. He did just that on the inbound pass, giving one of their guards a one-and-one free throw. But we were still ahead by three points with only one or two seconds to go. Our lead fell to two when their shooter sank the first free throw. Then, he deliberately missed the second one.

I still remember clearly the sinking feeling in the pit of my stomach when the ball took a "lucky St. Henry" bounce directly to their center, and he rebounded it in to tie the game at the buzzer. Although we scored a few points during the overtime period, they won by one or two. That loss was the hardest for me of any I ever experienced at any level.

* * *

I was not as shy in high school as when I was ten and younger, but I was still practically speechless around girls. Through my sophomore year, I rarely participated in any social events outside school hours, other than playing basketball and baseball. In my spare time at home, I read mainly about sports, played my APBA baseball game, and played lots of baseball and basketball with Jim, as well as baseball against the Burkettsville team in the summer on our home diamond.

My best friends in school during those years were two of my teammates, Ed Kemper and Jon Betz. In the class behind me, Jon was a bright guy and a pretty good basketball player. He lived a few blocks from the high school, and I sometimes went with him to his house at noon for lunch. As a sophomore, he was interested in calculus and studied it for a while on his own.

I was impressed with that, and Jon was impressed when I won the American Legion Essay Contest two years in a row. I told him few students entered in spite of the $20 first prize, so he should give it a try. I don't think he ever entered. Jon was much more of a social rebel than I was, so the kind of patriotic essay the judges were looking for came more naturally to me than to him.

Most of the basketball players in my class and the next two shared my shyness around girls. In my junior year, someone decided some of us players should be escorts for the homecoming queen's court. It involved a dance after the game, and that was too much for us. We all showered quickly when the game ended and hurried off to a downtown restaurant. The girls in the court were matched with other, more socially adept, escorts – no doubt a fortunate outcome for them. The adult homecoming organizers later frowned and grumbled at my teammates and me, but I don't remember any punishment.

Mostly I was a serious and conforming student, but uncharacteristically I got in trouble a couple of times as a sophomore. One of these events happened on a bird-watching field trip in biology class. For the field trip our teacher, Mr. Max Johnson, arranged for members of his biology class to be excused from their other morning classes up to 10:00 or 10:30 am. At around 7:00 am, class members met Mr. Johnson at a woods owned by a local farmer who agreed to allow us to look for birds on his land.

Our instructions were to go off in groups of four or five into the woods and record the names of all birds we saw. Then meet back at the starting location before returning to school and our other classes. My group ventured away from the rest of the class as quickly as we could and mainly wasted time rather than look seriously for birds.

We were several miles away when the class met to return to school. At first, it was daring and fun to be out of school but within an hour, we were getting bored and a little scared about our consequences. We walked the mile or two to school arriving around lunch time to learn some of the other bird-watching groups were also late getting to school.

Later that day or the next, Doc Knapke met with all ten or twelve of us delinquents to express his displeasure with our behavior and assign a week of after-school detentions to each of us. I think Doc was unusually lenient because he partially blamed Mr. Johnson for not managing the class better. A detention was a little embarrassing for me, but it only involved spending an hour after school in a quiet classroom supervised by a teacher. I used the time to study or read.

On another morning that year, the hall was full of students milling around waiting for the bell to ring signaling the beginning of classes. Ed Kemper and I were standing and talking near the fire alarm, joking about ringing it and wondering how it was done. A vertical metal handle, about the size and shape of the handle of a broom or pitchfork, ran to the floor from a bell attached to the wall about eight feet high.

As we speculated about how to activate the alarm, Ed was checking out the vertical handle. He grabbed it with both hands and pushed down firmly, hitting accidentally on the formula for activation. Ed and I were shocked, but there was nothing we could do to stop the students and teachers from following the school's fire alarm protocol and filing out of the building as the fire bell clanged loudly. Soon after the building was emptied, a truck from the Fort Recovery Fire Department pulled up, and firemen silenced the alarm bell and checked the building for signs of fire. They declared a false alarm.

In panic, I told Ed we needed to confess what we had done. He was not as sure as I was, but with a little prodding he agreed. He and I talked to Principal Knapke, explaining we had activated the alarm but had not intended to. He sternly admonished us, noting that setting a false fire alarm was a federal offense. At first I had visions of going to jail, but Doc's tone soon softened. Our penalty was to report for after-school detentions for a week or two. After serving one or two days of detention, we were allowed to check in with the detention supervisor each of the remaining days and go on to basketball practice. It turned out to be a pretty light penalty for a federal offense.

* * *

Future Farmers of America officers in my junior year: beginning 2nd from left: Jerry Schoen, Fred Schmitz, Leo Schwieterman, Oscar Jutte. Harry Schoen is on right.

By my junior year, my classmates and I had our driver licenses and were ready to begin a little more active social life. A good friend from some of my classes, Oscar Jutte, enjoyed movies as much as I did. We recruited a group of other guys to join us for a movie on either Saturday or Sunday night most weekends. Harry and Jerry were nearly always included, and usually one or two other friends joined us. We attended a movie from the seven or eight choices within about a 25-mile radius, and we usually stopped for a hamburger and soft drink afterwards.

In the late summer when county fairs were running in the area, we often spent the evening at a fair instead of a movie. This sort of social evening was typical for me for a couple of years, until I left home for college. I didn't drink anything alcoholic until after high school, and I never took up smoking although it was common among college students at the time. After graduating from high school, instead of a night at a movie this same group of friends usually started at a local bar for a beer or sloe gin fizz before going on to a dance.

In my summers during high school Fritz Kunkler hired me to help run his farm at busy times while he worked fulltime at New Idea. I also took other jobs on near-by farms when Dad and Fritz didn't need me. The pay was not much but the work was pretty steady, and it gave me a little pocket change for movies and other recreation.

* * *

In November of my freshman year, my five-year-old brother Rick was feeling sick with a pain in his lower abdomen. Mom and Dad always put off taking their children to the doctor as long as possible, partly because they had no medical insurance. Ordinarily, this was not a problem as we were an unusually healthy group. Dad trusted the medical advice of the Fort Recovery pharmacist, Ted Sauer, and for a week or more Rick took medicine recommended by Ted but continued to get worse.

Finally, Rick was so low on a Sunday morning Dad and Mom decided they had to take him to see Dr. Harnick in Coldwater. They had stopped going to Dr. Heurkamp because the nuns who operated the Coldwater Hospital did not allow him to practice there. Mom who was expecting her last child Dave in about six weeks, wanted to take a group of her children to late mass, so Dad and Kate took Rick to see the doctor.

Kate remembers Dr. Harnick told them Rick had appendicitis and his appendix needed to be removed immediately. They took him directly to the hospital where Dad stayed with him while Kate went home so Mom could go to be with Rick, too. His appendix had ruptured, and he was in serious condition for nearly a week after his operation.

Never having had any major health problems in the family, we all worried and prayed a lot until Rick's condition improved. His care was demanding on the time of my parents and older sisters. At five years old, he needed an adult in the family to be with him nearly all the time during his two-week hospital stay. After he got home, he required special attention for months before he got back to full strength.

Some of 65-year-old Rick's memories of the incident follow. "I remember looking forward to the food on Thanksgiving that year and then being too sick to eat anything. I have only vague memories of being in the hospital; scary machines and people in gowns. I do remember getting special treats after I was home; more ice cream than normal and lots of people taking care of me. It was a close call, and I'm lucky they took me in when they did." The medical costs related to the illness, while small compared to today's prices, must have put a strain on our family's already shaky financial situation.

* * *

With few exceptions like teachers, doctors and priests, the adults in my experience had at most a high school education and many did not finish high school. At the time, opportunities for employment in the area, besides farming, were mostly agricultural business and industry, jobs for which post-secondary education was not required. To my knowledge no one in my relationship prior to my generation all the way back to Germany had ever gone to college.

My parents' attitudes about education had grown to the point they were OK with their children graduating from high school, but post-secondary education was another matter. After her high school graduation, Ginny seriously considered going to Dayton for a nursing program but with no family support, financial or otherwise, she decided instead to stay at home and work as office manager at St. Clair Mills in Fort Recovery.

Since no one in our extended family had experience in higher education, I was on my own when it came to decisions about college. Mom and Dad did not discourage me, but they were of no help either. One big boost for me came in my sophomore year when Doc Knapke invited three or four of his top mathematics students to go with him to Ohio State University's Engineering Day in Columbus.

Tom Bubp, Bob Diller, and I, all sophomores, were included

and perhaps a junior, Jim Kramer. We visited Engineering classes and laboratories, listened to speakers talk about careers in Engineering, and gathered information about OSU's Engineering programs. This was a completely new world for me, but I might learn to fit into it. To add to the day's effect, most of the conversation in the car to and from Columbus was about college and Engineering, conversations like none I'd ever participated in. I realized my fellow students in the car would go to college, and they were no better students than I was. The day was an eye-opening experience enabling me to imagine a future other than farming or working at the New Idea.

I was fortunate to be in school when attitudes about college education were changing, even in rural areas like Mercer and Darke County. The nation's economy was strong and advances in technology were increasing the level of education needed for many jobs with good pay and benefits. The cost of postsecondary education was much more reasonable than it later became. As they got older, Mom and Dad too developed an appreciation for the value of education. My impression was Mom would have stayed in school longer were it not for family pressures.

When Mom was nearly 100 years old, she was interviewed for a school project by one of her great grandchildren. She told a number of stories about the fun she had in school, including being the pitcher on the softball team and a member of a volleyball team that was "pretty good for a small school." She was proud of "The

Mom in 1957; I'm not sure who the clown is behind her.

115

encouragement Teacher Burke gave me when I helped teach the younger kids. He said I was a natural born teacher and should think of becoming a teacher," after which she hesitated, thought for a second, then smiled and added wryly, "Oh, well."

When I was a junior, some of my classmates were talking about college. Oscar Jutte, whose father was a successful farmer, was planning to go to Ohio State to study agricultural economics. Some of the better mathematics and science students like Tom Bubp and Bob Diller, my future brother-in-law Neil's older brother, were thinking about majoring in engineering or one of the sciences.

I was interested in college by then, too, but I had no idea how I could manage it. Some of my teachers mentioned scholarships, grants, and loans, but I had only a vague understanding of what these were and no idea how to get such awards. Toward the end of junior year, my college prospects changed for the better, although I wasn't aware of it at the time. Doc Knapke announced Bob Fiely would be FRHS basketball and baseball coach the next year.

6 SENIOR YEAR

The first two weddings in the Arnold and Rose Schoen family took place in the summer before my senior year. Ginny married Bill Boeckman in June, and Janice married Harold Hemmelgarn in September. Both the weddings were traditional for Catholic families in Sharpsburg. A wedding mass in the morning at St. Paul's was followed by a photo session and lunch for the immediate families at someone's home or in a small church hall.

The wedding reception was in a much larger hall with a capacity of three or four hundred people, which was about the number of uncles, aunts, cousins, neighbors, and school friends who were invited. The reception typically started at 2:00 or 3:00 in the afternoon. The families of the wedding couple always provided an unlimited supply of beer and soft drinks for everyone.

After visiting for a few hours and eating a huge supper around 5:00 pm, most of the guests went home to their farms to do the evening chores. They came back to the reception hall around 8:00 pm for a night of fun and dancing. Square dancing and other group dancing like the Bunny Hop were particular favorites. The party usually continued until midnight or a little later.

* * *

Sports were a big part of my high school experience from the start, and since my sophomore year I had been thinking of going to college. It appeared sports may help me do that. By the start of my senior year, I was 6'6" tall and weighed about 170 pounds. I continued to enjoy playing baseball and to be a fan of major league baseball, but any future I had in college sports was in basketball.

Through my junior year, no one had ever suggested I could play Division I college basketball with a full athletic scholarship, but the coach at Defiance, Ohio, College, a pretty good Division III program, wondered if I was interested in partial financial support to play there. I was flattered by the interest, but I never followed up.

In my senior year, school activities including sports dominated my time just as they had in previous years. Besides the weekend movie group I described in the previous chapter, my social life revolved around the sporting events in which I participated. I still enjoyed recreational reading, but I had lost interest in playing my APBA game. My shyness with girls was sometimes painful, but it was partly a good thing as I had little money and the boy always paid on dates.

With the end of high school rapidly approaching I could no longer put off serious consideration of my future. Fortunately, the school year went well for me in nearly every way, and as the year progressed my plans began to fall into place. My new coach provided a great deal of help with those plans.

I was impressed with Coach Bob Fiely. He was a childhood hero of mine, and in real life he struck me as a modest, even-tempered man who had to be prompted to talk about his substantial sports accomplishments. When he arrived at FRHS, he had recently completed his two-year military commitment following his Reserve Officer Training Corps (ROTC) program at the University of Dayton. He was a firm disciplinarian, but he hardly had to assert himself to get the desired effect on student behavior. My teammates and I were pleased to have him as our coach, and our team records in both baseball and basketball were the best of my high school career.

The greatest thing for me was he began to talk to me early in the basketball season about playing at UD the following year. At first, I questioned Coach Fiely and myself about whether I was good enough to play at that level. He said I would improve with the tougher competition and not to worry. He had played there, and he should know. I was not convinced he was right for a long time, but it was the best opportunity I had to pay for a college education. I'd be foolish not to pursue it.

* * *

I had been reading about college and professional basketball regularly for several years in *Sport* magazine articles, and since I may become a college player my interest increased. One tragic story was about the point-shaving scandal in 1951 that involved players from the University of Kentucky as well as some New York City area college teams.

I was reminded of the Chicago Black Sox baseball scandal I read about earlier in which eight members of the Chicago White Sox cooperated with gamblers to make sure the Cincinnati Reds won the 1919 World Series. At the time, I couldn't imagine why anyone who played on a team would deliberately play poorly, or, for that matter, how they could keep their coaches and teammates from recognizing their lack of effort.

In the 1940s and early 1950s, there were several postseason collegiate basketball tournaments. The most prestigious one was the National Invitation Tournament (NIT) played in New York City's Madison Square Garden, sometimes called the Mecca of college basketball. During the 1950s and early 1960s, the NIT continued to be competitive with the newer NCAA tournament, and some teams including the UD Flyers declined invitations to the NCAA tournament to participate in the NIT.

In 1970, the NCAA effectively put an end to any possibility of a competitive post-season NIT by ruling a college basketball team that turned down an invitation to the NCAA tournament could not participate in any other post-season tournament. The prestige of the NIT also suffered as the number of teams in the tournaments expanded over the years. In the early sixties, the NCAA was a 16-team tournament, and the NIT fielded 12 teams. By 2015, 64 of the nation's best teams were invited to the postseason NCAA, leaving the NIT's 32 slots to be filled from the remaining pool of teams.

As I described in Chapter 4, my interest in college basketball spiked in 1953-54 when UD sophomore Bob Fiely began to play for the Flyers varsity team. The Flyers competed in the NIT in each of Fiely's three varsity years. While the Flyers had much of my attention in those years, I couldn't help but notice the University of San Francisco Dons, NCAA Tournament champions in 1955 and 1956. With Bill Russell, their amazingly talented 6'9" star, they were changing the game of college basketball.

Through 1955, the free throw lane was six feet wide with an offensive player given one of the inside rebounding positions which for the Dons was occupied by Bill Russell when one of his teammates was shooting. The other Dons deliberately missed free throws on Russell's side of the basket allowing him to grab the rebound and score two points instead of one. When the Dons had the ball out of bounds under their own basket, the player passing the ball inbounds arched it high over the backboard so it came down near the basket where Russell jumped above the defensive players and dunked the ball.

In 1956, the NCAA made several rule changes designed to neutralize Russell's height and skills to some extent. The changes included doubling the width of the free-throw lane from six to twelve feet, giving both inside rebounding positions on free throws to the defensive team, and prohibiting an in-bounds pass from under a team's offensive basket that went over the backboard. These changes were adopted in high school basketball, too, beginning in my sophomore year (1956-57).

As for professional basketball, the NBA was formed in 1947 and was still struggling to establish itself in the 1950s. In their first decade, salaries were so meager many good players left the league after a year or two to seek greener pastures. The best NBA team in the early 1950s was the Minneapolis Lakers who had the first superstar big man, 6'10" George Mikan. In the late 1950s, the Boston Celtics, led by Bill Russell, began their phenomenal run of 11 NBA championships in 13 years. In 1960, the Minneapolis Lakers moved to Los Angeles where they continued their winning tradition over the years to the present with such great players as Jerry West, Elgin Baylor, Wilt Chamberlain, Kareem Abdul-Jabbar, Magic Johnson, Shaquille O'Neal, and Kobe Bryant.

* * *

My senior year stands out in my mind as a year of transition and maturation. Teachers and younger students had a special respect for the seniors and their accomplishments. I was an A or A- student for my first three years and that continued in my senior year. I did well in all areas of study and best in mathematics. I don't remember ever getting less than A in a grading period in a high school math course.

At FRHS, there was no accelerated math track. Like everyone in the college prep track, I took Algebra I as a freshman, Plane Geometry as a sophomore, and Algebra II as a junior. Algebra II was offered every other year, alternating with a semester of Solid Geometry and a semester of Trigonometry, two courses I took in my senior year. At that time, it was common for students with a high school background like mine to take a semester of College Algebra and a semester of Trigonometry as college freshmen to reinforce and slightly extend their knowledge in these areas.

Elementary Calculus did not begin until sophomore year in college, and some colleges offered a separate Analytic Geometry course taken prior to Calculus as well. Students who had gone to strong academic high schools may be accelerated by a semester or a year, but that was the exception not the rule.

One of the few frustrations in my senior classes was on a Physics class assignment. After we studied how radio transmission worked, Mr. Price's assignment was for each of us to build our own working radio. Some of my classmates bought kits with the needed materials, but I couldn't afford that so I used rough materials from Dad's workshop. They did not work at all. After several tries, I was not picking up any radio signals. Faced with the assignment deadline, my radio was still not working, but Mr. Price came around to my desk, put his ear close to the radio and declared he could hear static. I was off the hook, but only because of Mr. Price's generosity.

When class rankings were determined, I was fourth in the class of 44, and I won two of the main awards or keys for boys in the class. (First cousin Betty Miller was valedictorian.) I was awarded the Boys' Athletic Key because I had earned nine varsity letters, more than any other boy in my class. I had other accomplishments like membership in the National Honor Society, representing the school in state testing competitions each year usually in a mathematical subject, and winning the American Legion Essay Contest. These activities combined with my sports participation earned me the Boys' Activity Key.

In the 1959 FRHS yearbook, I am pictured with my tallest girl classmate as winners of the, pretty meaningless, boy and girl "Tallest" in the class awards. Ed Kemper won the "Wittiest Boy" award, and we often kidded each other over the years about those two awards.

The senior honor that most surprised me came when the junior class elected me King of the Senior Prom. The prom king was usually a popular, outgoing guy who was involved in lots of socially visible activities like plays or class offices, and I didn't fit the mold. I was a little embarrassed at first, but I felt better when my classmates were supportive and complimentary. Fortunately, I had gotten over some of my shyness around girls and had a good time in my royal role at the prom.

For me, our senior class trip to Washington, D. C., was a memorable culmination to a great school year. We took a bus to Cincinnati where we caught an overnight passenger train to Washington, my first time on a train and the furthest I had been from home. We stayed in Washington for

In Washington hotel lobby wondering if I would ever stay in an exotic place like this again.

two nights in a nice hotel, another first for me. It was great fun on the train as the current pop hit *The Battle of New Orleans* sung by Johnny Horton blared again and again on my classmates' radios. "In 1814, we took a little trip, along with Colonel Jackson down the mighty Mississip."

Mr. Williams, our chaperone, enjoyed himself as much as we did, and some of us spent quite a lot of time talking to him. Seeing the Smithsonian, the Capitol, the White House and other sites of Washington is a blur to me now as I have been there scores of times since, but I'm sure I was completely overwhelmed at the time.

* * *

Our baseball team was strong that year, winning about two-thirds of our games. My pitching and hitting had improved considerably. I often pitched complete seven-inning games sometimes with strikeouts in double digits, including a one-hitter in the spring. My batting average was .296, second on the team, and I hit several doubles and a triple. The triple came against the best pitcher in the MCL who I had had trouble hitting since he pitched fast-pitch softball in eighth grade. I never played organized baseball after high school, but I loved the game as is clear in these memories of my triple I wrote in the summer of 1971.

Their left-handed pitcher was the fastest in the league. He often struck out 15 or more batters in a seven-inning game. Hal's batting average was just over .250, and he was scared – no, petrified – to face this pitcher. The count went to two and oh when the first two pitches just missed, outside. Hal dug in for the next pitch, knowing it would be a fastball. As it came like a rocket toward the heart of the plate, Hal swung with all his might. The contact of leather and hardwood was exhilarating. The recoil of the bat as it made solid contact with the center of the ball told him this time he had a hit. It was a line drive smash into right center field between the outfielders.

As Hal raced around the bases, legs pumping madly, his mind was racing, too. For this moment, he wasn't just a small town high school baseball player. He was a major leaguer, a most valuable player, a superstar, a hall of famer. After the game, he would go home to his family's farm, milk the cows and feed the pigs, but for now the world was the baseball field and Hal was on top of it.

Our basketball team was a local power, finishing 19-3 and winning the MCL season and tournament championships. It was an enjoyable senior season packed with many pleasant memories. I had my best year individually averaging over 19 points per game while hitting 60% from the field and 76% from the free throw line and earning a spot on the all-MCL first team, but my classmate Leo Schwieterman did even better. He was the top scorer in the MCL at around 23 points per game.

1959 FRHS Indians; first row, l to r: Tom Berry, Bob Diller, Jerry Kaiser, Rich Newell; 2nd row: Dave Williams, Jon Betz, me, Leo Schwieterman, Ed Kemper, Coach Bob Fiely

Other starters were Ed, Jon Betz, and sophomore Dave Williams. Because of Leo's success, opposing teams could not focus their defense on me as they had in the previous two years. Our team also made up, to some extent, for the tough loss to St. Henry the previous year by beating them three times, twice during the season and again in the MCL tournament.

The game I remember best from senior year is the MCL tournament finals against Marion Local. We lost one early non-conference season game by one-point to New Bremen, but we were undefeated in the MCL until the last game of the season at Marion Local. Marion Local was in second place with two MCL losses including a close one to us in Fort Recovery.

We clinched the league title before that last game, but it was painfully embarrassing to lose by around 20 points leaving us with a season record of 16-2. We shook off the defeat and cruised to the MCL tournament final game without much challenge. Marion Local met with similar success in their tournament games, setting the stage for a rubber game in the finals between what were clearly the two best teams in the MCL that year.

Both teams played well in the final game, and it was close throughout. I played one of the best offensive games of my high school career, scoring steadily from close range during the first half. When Marion changed their defense at half time to deny me the ball inside, I went out to the corner and consistently hit jumpers and set shots from there. Years later, Bucky Albers, a *Dayton Daily News* sports reporter who was assigned to our championship game, told me he was impressed enough with my size and ability to play both inside and outside to recommend me to UD Flyer coach, Tom Blackburn. I scored 27 points, but Marion Local did not go down easily. The score was tied at the end of the game and again at the end of the first overtime.

The rule at the time was the second overtime was "sudden death," that is, the first team to score won the game. It was extremely important for a team to get the ball on the tip-off that opened the "sudden death" period. Marion Local's center was about my height, and he had gotten up quickly that night to get the previous tip-offs against me. Confident they would get the ball on this tip-off as well, their coach instructed his guard who was positioned in the backcourt to leave our basket and race toward their end of the court when the referee tossed the ball in the air intending to get a "three on one" or "three on two" situation against our guards.

Knowing how crucial it was to get the tip, I jumped as the ball was going up, this time beating their center to it. I tipped it forward to Jon Betz who passed it to Leo as he ran down the court and laid the ball into our basket. We were the 1959 MCL tournament champions.

It was a satisfying win and great to be a member of a

championship team, but we could only enjoy the euphoria for a day or two. Then it was time to prepare for our first district tournament game the next weekend, a re-match against New Bremen. We had improved since our early season loss to them, so we thought we had a good chance of winning. Unfortunately, it was not to be as we played poorly against a good team and lost by 18 points.

In Spring of my senior year, a first-year teacher, Mr. Cotner, started a track team. It was completely new to me, but I did pretty well in the high jump, winning in one or two meets. I think I was jumping around 5'10" at my best. I went to the state meet, but I did not jump as well there as I had in earlier meets. I participated in track just enough as a senior to wish I'd had the opportunity in earlier years.

* * *

In October or November that year, I drove to Dayton with some classmates to a site where the SAT was administered. At the time, I wasn't sure if the UD basketball opportunity would materialize, and a possible alternative was General Motors Institute (GMI) in Flint, Michigan. GMI offered engineering programs in which students worked and went to school in alternate semesters with the money earned at work paying for the education. Due largely to Doc Knapke's influence, engineering was my main interest, and GMI provided a way for me to earn the educational expenses.

In December, Coach Fiely took me to Dayton to see a Flyer basketball game and to meet their coach. I had never seen a Flyer game live, but I knew all about the Flyers. Tom Blackburn, a former World War II naval officer, had been the Flyers coach since 1947. With mainly local and regional high school talent, he coached the Flyers to national prominence during the 1950s. His teams had competed seven times in the NIT in Madison Square

Garden and finished second five times. Bob Fiely was a member of two of those NIT runner-up teams.

I saw the Flyers play often on television, and I regularly watched the *Tom Blackurn Show* each Sunday afternoon during the basketball season. On his television show, he smiled a lot and came across as a personable gentleman, though I had heard from friends of Bob Fiely when he was a Flyer that Coach Blackburn was very demanding with his players. I'm not sure why, but Bob never talked to me about Blackburn's tough side other than to say he was a firm disciplinarian or words to that effect.

I met Tom Blackburn at half-time of the freshman game. College freshmen were not eligible to play on the varsity at that time, so the freshman team played another college freshmen team or a local semi-professional or amateur team as a preliminary to each home varsity game. Coach Blackburn made a positive comment about my height, but most of the conversation was about an exciting player on the freshman team that year, 6'6" Garry Roggenburk.

I was impressed to see Garry dribble the length of the court at top speed and dunk the ball. At the time, few men his size could handle the ball so well. Garry was not only an outstanding basketball player but also a left-handed pitching ace who had turned down a large major league baseball bonus at high school graduation to attend UD. In basketball, Garry drove well to the basket and had an amazingly accurate running left-handed hook shot, but his jump shot was pretty awkward and erratic.

It says a lot about college basketball at the time that Coach Blackburn was working with Garry, not to improve his jump shot, but rather to develop a two-handed set shot. At the time, Tom much preferred his players take one- or two-handed set shots rather than jump shots, as he thought a jump shooter was off-balance. I never heard him admit as much, but I expect coaching unsuccessfully three times against Oscar Robertson and the University of Cincinnati from 1958 through 1960 convinced him at least some jump shooters were effective.

Oscar (aka the "Big O") was the top college player of the era and one of the best, most versatile basketball players of all time. The Big O had an accurate and nearly unstoppable jump shot, but he was far more than just a shooter. As an illustration of what he could do, consider a triple double *in a single game* (that is, ten or more each of points, rebounds and assists) is pretty rare in the NBA and is considered a noteworthy mark of versatility for a player. Across the first five seasons of his NBA career (1960-65), Oscar *averaged per game* over 30 points, over 10 rebounds and over 10 assists, an incredible record of all-around mastery of the game no one has come close to matching. He did this while playing a combination of today's "point guard" and "shooting guard."

Knowing about the Big O and UD standouts like Garry Roggenburk, I was amazed to be considered as a potential major college player. Yet that spring the UD Flyers offered me a full scholarship that covered all tuition, fees, room, board, and books. Nothing was written down and few specifics were even spoken, but I understood the scholarship was contingent on my making the freshman team and later the varsity.

My scholarship could be taken away at any time, but I was pleased to have it as I had no good alternative to pay for college. Later, I learned from my freshman teammates seven or eight of the most highly recruited of them had written four-year guaranteed scholarships. At any rate, I was one of 15 or 16 UD freshmen on a basketball scholarship at the beginning of the 1959-60 school year.

Having the scholarship was a relief and a worry to me. It was a relief to know I'd be attending the University of Dayton and my scholarship would pay for it. I expected to do fine in my classes at UD but the worry, and it was huge for me at the time, was I wouldn't make the team. Fort Recovery High School was a small school compared to the schools where many of my UD freshman teammates had played, and my high school basketball record was not as outstanding as most of theirs.

At best, I had a long way to go to show I could be an asset to the Dayton Flyers. Partly in response to this worry, I decided to switch my major to high school mathematics teaching after Coach Fiely warned me it'd be difficult to be a UD basketball player and an engineering major with many late afternoon labs. In retrospect, I'm sure this was the right decision for me. I was more comfortable with the idea of being a teacher than an engineer, as I had many teacher models in my life but no engineers.

* * *

In the spring and summer of my senior year, the worry of making the team was never far from my mind though it was overshadowed by the realization I was going to be leaving home and living in a city for the first time. The adjustment to UD and campus life in Dayton, whatever happened in basketball, was going to be hard. It was some consolation to talk about my worries with my friend Oscar who had similar concerns about attending Ohio State University that fall. Sometime during our many conversations about the matter, Oscar and I agreed to keep in touch regularly by letter and try to be of some support to each other during the fall semester.

In March, Dad and Mom sold the west 40 acres of our farm to neighbor Albert Weitzel leaving them with just 57 acres. With so little land to farm, it was a good thing I got a full-time job that summer at St. Clair Mills, a big feed mill in Fort Recovery. Ginny had been part-time office manager there since her sophomore or junior year in high school, becoming full-time after she graduated. My sister Pat assisted Ginny part-time during her high school years and took over full-time after Ginny married and started her family.

Pat remembers, "Ginny was always a planner. She was going to get married, so she began to train me to take over her job." Pat also appreciated what a good teacher Ginny was and how much

St. Clair Mills in the 1950s

she taught her about bookkeeping and the feed mill business. St. Clair Mills owner, Dick Staugler, was impressed with the quality of the work both of them did and often mentioned how lucky he was to have them at St. Clair Mills.

During her freshman and sophomore years, Pat walked to the Mill after school and then rode home after work with Kate who was office manager at Les Wenning Ford, also in Fort Recovery. After Kate got married in Pat's junior year she had no ride home, so she used some of the wages she had saved to buy a 1950 Oldsmobile. She remembers taking carloads of friends to away basketball games in her last two years of school when Jim was a FRHS varsity regular as a freshman and sophomore.

Most days that summer I saw my sisters briefly in the office, but I mostly helped to deliver truckloads of 80-pound bags of ground feed to farmers in the area. Lifting those bags was hard work that helped to improve my strength. The wages I earned provided me with spending money for the school year in Dayton, and the summer work schedule helped keep my mind off my concerns about the upcoming school year.

I also played slow-pitch softball on a Sharpsburg team in a Sunday afternoon league that summer. Ed Kemper played on the St. Joe team in the same league, and he called games between our teams "Battles of the Mastodons." It was great fun, and I played on the Sharpsburg team for the next five summers. Into

131

my early forties, I spent many enjoyable summer hours playing slow-pitch softball in various town or intramural leagues, including two summers on a team in Dayton in the late 1960s with Ed at first base while I covered the outfield with my brothers, Jim and Rick.

As my high school sports career was winding down, Jim was showing clear potential to be an outstanding high school baseball and basketball player. By the time he was in junior high, Sharpsburg and the other small schools in the area had merged with Fort Recovery to form the Southwest School District. In his eighth-grade year (my senior year), Jim began to play on the district's junior high basketball team that practiced and played in the FRHS gym.

When Jim started to play, Dad's pessimism came out as it had when I first went out for basketball. Dad questioned him, not about the town boys as he had me, but instead asked, "Do you think you will ever be as good as Harold?" Whatever sibling rivalry there was between Jim and me came out in good ways as we continued to practice both sports together at home in those years.

In the summers after my junior and senior years, Jim and I often borrowed a car from Dad or one of our older sisters so we could go to Fort Recovery in the evening after milking to play pick-up basketball games with some of my FRHS teammates or whoever else was interested and available. We played on the outdoor blacktop court at the Catholic School. After our games, all hot and sweaty, we usually stopped at Brum's Grocery Store on our way out of Fort Recovery to get several of our favorite soft drinks or sometimes a cold watermelon.

In late August 1959, my sister Eileen's wedding to Carl Barhorst was a nice occasion, but the family had a scare at the reception when one of my uncles got drunk and drove off with my four-year-old brother Dave asleep in the backseat of his car. We were all in a panic, not knowing where Dave was, until my

Rick and his four oldest brothers-in-law, l to r : Junior Thornton (Kate), Harold Hemmelgarn (Janice), Bill Boeckman (Ginny), Carl Barhorst (Eileen)

uncle finally sobered up enough to bring him to our house.

In spite of this scare, I had a good time at the reception. It was my first night of drinking beer. As I mentioned earlier, I rarely had a beer in high school but at Eileen's wedding, just a few weeks before I was scheduled to report for registration at UD, I was in a mood to drown my worries about the future. I had a great time, and I was fortunate to have no hangover the next morning.

A couple of weeks later, I took my loosely packed suitcase and the old Underwood typewriter my parents gave me for college and caught my 60-mile ride to Dayton with FRHS classmate, Bob Diller, who was enrolled at UD as an engineering major. When I think of going off to college for the first time, I am reminded of the warning yell in a hide-and-seek game: "Here I come, ready or not."

7 COLLEGE

I doubt there was ever a college freshman more homesick than me in my first few weeks at UD that fall of 1959. Born and raised on our family farm, I never lived anywhere else. I rarely slept in a bedroom other than the one I shared for years with my brothers. Life in a city, even in a small town, was completely foreign to me. I traveled further than a hundred miles from home just once, on my senior class trip. It is still painful for me to recall my loneliness and misery, beginning on the first day of registration.

Before computer registration became common in the 1970s and 1980s, UD, like many colleges and universities, filled their basketball court with rows of tables and assigned each academic program a space at one of the tables for two or three days of registration just prior to the start of the semester's classes. Students planned a course schedule for the semester with a faculty advisor in their major field, which often included courses in four or five different academic programs.

Students then stood in line at each of these programs' registration locations to get a class card to verify their membership in the class. The lines were often long and slow, and late in the registration period one or more of the desired courses may be filled requiring a re-thinking of the student's entire schedule. Never having navigated anything like this system, I was intimidated to say the least.

After waiting in a long line to work out a class schedule with my new advisor in the College of Education, I happened to mention my basketball scholarship. What followed was my first experience with the privilege that came with being a member of the Flyers basketball team. After asking me with great interest about my high school basketball career, my advisor went off to find Herbie Dintamin, the freshman basketball coach who I had not yet met. Herbie was cordial and supportive.

He checked my course schedule and noted I had signed up for Army ROTC. At that time, a minimum of two years of ROTC was required of all male students. Herbie asked me if I wanted to take ROTC, and I said, "No, but I thought it was required." He asked, "How tall are you?" and noted at 6'7" I was an inch taller than the army's height limit. Herbie took me to the ROTC table where my height was measured, and I was given a waiver.

Herbie also collected the cards I needed for my other courses. In future semesters, I turned my course schedule in to Herbie's office, and my cards were pulled in advance of regular registration. UD basketball players thus avoided the registration lines and the possibility of full classes other students had to face each semester.

So my first registration worked out well, thanks to Herbie, but my dorm assignment was another matter. An anxious, homesick freshman introvert from a hardscrabble Darke County farm, I was assigned to live in St. Joseph Hall with a sophomore varsity basketball player roommate who I will call Sam.

Sam was on academic probation. There were an odd number of varsity players to be paired as roommates in St. Joseph Hall, so Sam was singled out for a freshman roommate. This was awkward for both of us and to add to the awkwardness and to my loneliness, all the other freshman basketball players lived in a new dormitory that year, Founders Hall.

UD buildings l to r: St. Mary's Hall, Chapel of the Immaculate Conception, St. Joseph's Hall. The Fieldhouse is about 500 yards down the hill in front of St. Joe's Hall.

Herbie told me later I was the freshman recruit chosen to be Sam's roommate in the hope, as a good student, I'd have a positive influence on Sam and his grade problems. In fact, I was no influence at all. We were very different people. He had a closet full of expensive looking clothes and five or six pairs of shoes. I had a small fraction of his wardrobe, and what I had was much more modest.

I rarely saw him as he was out of the room every night, usually not getting in until after I was asleep. He slept late most mornings, often skipping classes. He was impressed, in a condescending way, at how much I studied, but he found it impossible to study himself. As a result, he failed to get the necessary 2.0 grade point average and was dismissed from UD at the end of fall Semester 1959.

I never saw Sam again after that semester, but two stories about him have survived in the shared memories of my Flyer teammates and me. One morning approaching noon, Sam was asleep in his lower bunk when Willie, the St. Joseph Hall custodian, unlocked the door to empty the wastebaskets. At a slim 6'8" and sleeping soundly with his mouth wide open, Sam was an imposing sight.

Not expecting to find anyone in the room, the startled Willie jumped back, ran out into the hall to the next room where I was visiting with a couple of teammates. We all had a hearty laugh, repeated often in the years since, when Willie yelled, "There's a dead man in there!"

As the second story is told, in the week before fall semester final examinations and facing likely dismissal from school because of low grades, Sam gained access to a copy of a final exam for one of his classes from a friend of his who stole it from the professor's office. Rather than work through the exam and study it to be sure of doing well, Sam procrastinated, deciding to look at it the morning before the 11:00 a.m. exam. But he overslept that morning, never even read the exam, and the rest is history.

A bright spot in that otherwise difficult period came in September or early October of my freshman year when Ed Kemper went to an optometrist in Dayton to be fitted for contact lenses. In their conversations, Ed mentioned a high school teammate of his wore glasses and was a freshman on the UD Flyers basketball team. To correct my near-sightedness I had worn glasses all my waking hours since sixth grade including for sports.

The optometrist, Les Powell, who was a rabid Flyer fan, told Ed to have me call for an appointment. He'd fit me for a pair of contact lenses, free of charge. I jumped at the idea, and Dr. Powell generously kept me fitted with contact lenses throughout my college basketball career. I continued to wear contacts until I was in my mid-fifties when they became too uncomfortable for me, and I decided to go back to glasses.

* * *

When classes started near the end of September, I began to get into a daily routine, keeping busy in class most of the day and studying in the library between classes and for several hours each evening. I arranged to get rides home on Fridays after my last class. I returned to Dayton as late as I could arrange a ride on either Sunday evening or early Monday morning. At first, it was hard for me to go back to my comparatively lonely life at UD after a relaxing and social weekend at home.

After a few weeks, I was beginning to enjoy some of my classes and my quiet study time in Dayton. I also liked the cafeteria food, although most of the male students in the dormitory complained about it. UD girls lived off campus as there were no dormitory facilities for girls until newly built Marycrest Hall opened in 1962-63, my senior year.

Just as I was getting comfortable with my schedule, basketball practice started on October 15, and I had to deal with a busier schedule and a more difficult adjustment. The freshmen practiced five afternoons a week from 3:30 to 5:30 in the UD Fieldhouse on a smaller court at the end of the main court used by the varsity. That practice schedule made going home for a weekend impractical if not impossible for me. Herbie also discouraged us from going home, believing it was better for our adjustments to college and to basketball to stay in Dayton on the weekends. He was right, but I was still homesick.

Living in a different dormitory, I had no contact with my freshmen teammates before the start of practices. Now I was thrust daily into two hours of competition with them. During the first several days of practice, about 25 players participated, including eight or ten "walk-ons" along with the players on scholarships. I was intensely nervous during the first few practices, fearing Herbie and my teammates would soon discover my presence there was a mistake. I wasn't any good.

Building in my mind with that fear was a desire to somehow get rid of the pressure and homesickness I felt. I definitely wanted to be a student at UD. Trying to play basketball was the mistake causing my unhappiness. I told myself I could find a part-time job and get loans to cover costs and still get back home when I felt the need. After brooding about what to do for a few days, I decided to quit the basketball team.

Fortunately, I didn't quit immediately. I felt bad to be letting Bob Fiely down after all he had done for me, so I wrote to tell him of my decision. I also wrote Oscar Jutte at Ohio State, and I called home and talked to Mom. Meanwhile, I said nothing to anyone in the UD basketball program and continued to attend practice.

My decision to quit somehow relieved some of my anxiety in practice, and I began to play a little better. There were about seven or eight four-year scholarship players who were definitely better than I was at the time, but I was competitive with the next group of five or six and better than another five or six. It slowly dawned on me my chances of making the freshman team were not as bleak as I thought at first.

Oscar phoned after he got my letter. Both he and Mom encouraged me to hang in there, and maybe things would improve. This was on a Wednesday or Thursday, and that Saturday, Ginny and her husband Bill drove to Dayton with Mom, Dad, and Jim. They picked me up at my dorm, and we spent several hours together talking about my decision. By the time they arrived in Dayton, I was feeling a lot better and leaning toward continuing with basketball after all. Their visit solidified my decision and confirmed I had love and support from my family.

Ginny had heard from a common friend that Bob Fiely said he thought I had more guts than to quit like this, and I decided he was right. I came through this trying episode firmly convinced I'd be a Dayton Flyer for four years or until Tom Blackburn told me otherwise. I'd get my college education paid for as long as possible, regardless of how low my fortunes on the basketball team may sink. I'd never again consider quitting. With this mindset, I faced practices with a renewed hope and determination, if not exactly confidence.

Freshmen practices at that time were pretty boring. Tom Blackburn believed anyone who was playing at this level had developed pretty good offensive skills in high school, but few players came to UD capable of playing defense well enough to suit him. He believed his and Herbie's job during our freshman year was to teach and practice defensive skills. His way of doing that was to restrict freshman practices to one-on-one half-court drills.

After explaining the basics of good individual defensive play in the first practice, Herbie put us through these repetitive one-on-one drills and yelled at us if we crossed our legs, went for a fake watching our opponent's head rather than his mid-section, failed to aggressively challenge a shot while avoiding a foul, failed to block our man out after he took a shot and on and on for the entire practice day after day. After a week or two, several walk-ons were cut and one or two scholarship players quit and went home, so the roster was down to around 15 players by the start of the season in early December.

As I mentioned in the previous chapter, the Flyer freshman team played another freshman college team or a local amateur or semi-pro team as a preliminary to each home varsity game. The freshman team also competed in the men's Amateur Athletic Union (AAU) league that played each Sunday afternoon at the Montgomery County Fairgrounds Coliseum, about a half-mile from the UD campus. These amateur teams had some outstanding players who were former high school or college stars, and they were more experienced and physically mature than we were. But we practiced every weekday we didn't play while they had day jobs, so we were in better physical condition. Our freshman team did well, winning about 70% of our games.

Herbie

Herbie Dintamin was gruff in practice and sometimes pushed us pretty hard, but he was a likable man who supported the players. He often played the "good cop" to Tom Blackburn's "bad cop." My teammates and I laughed a lot about his locker room talks. He always wanted us to run the five plays that comprised Coach Blackburn's simple offensive system, which we tried to do. Beyond that, Herbie, who had been a college football player, uttered platitudes like, "If you play good ball, you win. If you play bad ball, you lose." To try to get us to play better or harder, he accused us of playing like "a bunch of raggledy-assed cadets."

Through the month of December, I was doing A or B+ work in all my classes but basketball was not going so well. I was the fourth or fifth best forward on the team so I sat on the bench most of the time. When I got to play, it was usually near the end of a game whose outcome was already decided. My chances of making the Flyer varsity as a sophomore were looking pretty remote.

In fact, when Mom, Dad, and some of my siblings came to see an evening of Flyer freshman and varsity basketball shortly before Christmas, I introduced them to Herbie after our game. Herbie was gracious but uncomfortable. He told them I had a good attitude and was a good student, but it was awfully tough to come from as small a school as I did and play basketball at UD's level. He obviously was trying to prepare us for the likelihood I would not be invited to continue playing after my freshman year. It was hard for me to hear, but I wasn't surprised considering how little playing time I was getting.

Without warning over Christmas break, my future prospects improved. To begin, one of the starting forwards on our team had family problems and left school. A few days later, many of my freshman teammates who lived in Founders' Hall had a water battle. With no other students in the dorm over break they likely started it out of boredom with no malice intended, but the skirmish caused water damage in some of the rooms. The dormitory supervisor reported the incident to Herbie and then to Tom Blackburn.

The next day Tom and Herbie met with the freshman team in a Fieldhouse classroom. To hear him reading the riot act to the team, Tom Blackburn had never been more disgusted with the shocking behavior of a group of young men in his life. We all sat at our student desks uncomfortably looking down, wondering about our punishment.

After chewing us all out thoroughly, Blackburn snarled the names of two of my teammates and told them to get out, pack their bags, and go home. They were off the team. Period. And when they had gone, leaving the rest of us in shocked silence, Tom added with as much disdain in his voice as he could muster, *"And Schoen, you can thank your lucky stars you don't live in Founder's Hall or you'd be gone, too!"*

Blackburn had obviously used this incident as an opportunity to cut some players he didn't plan to keep anyway. There was no reason to think the players who were singled out were more to blame for the water battle than the more elite players on the team. I felt bad for the guys who were cut, but I did thank my "lucky stars" to still be on the team and now in a more important role.

Since the departing players were forwards, I became the first substitute forward. And Herbie also began to use me as the substitute center. My playing time increased significantly after the New Year. I got into games that were in contention, sometimes even in the first half. As a result, I became more comfortable on the court and scored and rebounded more regularly.

When the first semester ended in mid-January, my situation

on the team changed again. Unfortunately for him but not for me, our star forward went on grade probation and was ineligible to play during the second semester. In a matter of two or three weeks, by doing nothing but continue to show up and try my best, I went from a lowly bench warmer to a starting forward. For the remainder of the season, I played most of the time, starting at forward and moving to center as needed.

Junior & Kate Thornton

I don't remember much about individual freshman games, but one incident stands out in my mind. Kate was to marry Harvey Thornton, or Junior as the family calls him, on a Saturday in February that year (1960). They asked me to be their best man. I said I would if my coaches allowed me to miss the freshman game scheduled for that night. I asked Herbie, and as I feared, he checked with Tom.

I didn't know what to expect, thinking Tom may tell me to go home and stay there. But they agreed to allow my request after Tom instructed me firmly not to celebrate too much as those "Germans up north were likely to do at weddings." I had to be back in time to play in the Sunday afternoon AAU game. All went well at the wedding, and I was back in Dayton in plenty of time for the Sunday game.

We played a bad game and lost to a team that should not have beaten us. I did pretty well individually so no one blamed me, but Tom couldn't resist giving us static for the loss. The AAU teams were usually named for their business sponsor, like "Jones Brothers Mortuary." Tom had fun for a few days needling

Herbie and the team about our loss to a pushover opponent, which he sarcastically called the "Little Sisters of the Poor." Blackburn's ribbing aside, it was clear I had made tremendous progress over the season, scoring in low double figures in most games after I became a starter. I also continued to do well in my classes.

Meanwhile, the Flyer varsity accepted their invitation to the 1960 NIT. This meant the varsity had about a week of practice after the last game of the regular season to prepare for the tournament. As with his previous NIT teams, Tom invited the freshmen who would be on the varsity the next year to participate in practices during that week. I was nervous in the days leading up to Tom's invitation not knowing if I'd be included.

Three of my teammates on full four-year scholarships were sure to be invited. If Tom invited five players, I was "in" but if he only invited four it may be a toss-up between our other starting forward and me. When the list was posted, four players were on it, and much to my relief I was the fourth. The four of us were to play on the "scouting team" in varsity practices, mimicking the play of the varsity's first NIT opponent. More importantly, I would be on the varsity as a sophomore.

That week gave me some interesting insights into how much Coach Blackburn wanted to win the NIT after finishing second five times. The Flyers were invited to both the NCAA tournament and the NIT at least one of my freshman or sophomore years. Tom mentioned both invitations to the team and gave us a chance, sort of, to voice our opinion about which we should accept. It was always clear he much preferred the NIT, as he loved New York City and being a celebrity in Madison Square Garden.

He also had bad memories of the only NCAA Tournament game UD had played until then, an embarrassing 1952 loss against the University of Illinois on their court in which the

Flyers were called for a record number of personal fouls. Of course, we loved NYC, too, so the decision was a no-brainer. I sometimes wondered what Tom would do if the team insisted on going to the NCAA Tournament.

Each year in the first practice in preparation for the NIT, Tom showed us the last regulation time minute or two of the 35 mm black-and-white film of UD's overtime loss to Xavier in the final game of the 1958 NIT. Seeded UD had beaten XU handily twice during the 1957-58 season and XU was the twelfth and last team included in the NIT, but to everyone's surprise the Musketeers had an outstanding tournament. In the final game between UD and XU, the score was tied in the last few seconds of regulation play. As per Tom's plan for the last shot, the Flyers got the ball to center Jack McCarthy whose hook shot hit the back of the hoop, spun to the front, and out as the buzzer sounded. For the second or so the ball was on the rim, Tom was lost emotionally in that past moment. It was certainly obvious to his players; Tom Blackburn wanted very much to win the NIT.

Blackburn's practices were tense and serious. As a former World War II Naval officer, he expected nothing but the best effort from his players at all times, and his approach to getting that effort was to use his version of military discipline. He was stern, unyielding and caustic, never letting a player forget he was on a basketball scholarship and it was his responsibility to earn it. Woe to a player if Tom thought he wasn't playing his hardest. He often threatened to send someone back home if he didn't shape up.

Tom could and would humiliate a player verbally and make him run extra physically punishing drills. His sarcasm about what a lazy pushover someone was often continued for several days of practice, sometimes longer, depending on whether another player's failures caught his attention in the meantime. Outside practice, if he saw one of his targeted players he usually made a nasty remark about a basketball weakness. He never gave players positive feedback directly, although he sometimes made complimentary comments in the newspaper or on his television show. Thirsting for some sort of approval from our coach, we watched for those infrequent positive quotes and savored them.

During the pre-NIT week as a lowly freshman I was nervous, but it was good preparation for the following year. I remember being super-impressed with how hard and accurately Garry Roggenburk, a future major league pitcher, threw passes nearly the length of the court in our full-court fast break drills. When I was in high school, I didn't have "great hands", as they say, sometimes letting passes get away or opponents steal the ball. I soon found it took lots of concentration and tenacity just to hang onto Garry's hard passes, but I learned to do it. After that I rarely dropped a pass since none ever was as tough to handle as Garry's overhand, long-distance bullets.

One day, I inadvertently contributed to an incident that relieved the tension a bit in practice. Senior captain Frank Case was on the free throw line during a scrimmage, and I was in the inside rebounding position to the right of the basket. Frank was shooting two shots, but for some reason I thought it was a one-and-one. When he missed his first shot, I jumped up quickly and snared the rebound. Knowing he had another shot and my rebound was wasted effort, Frank mimicked the voice of the young boy in the last scene of the fifties blockbuster western *Shane* when the movie's star Alan Ladd rode off into the sunset as the boy pleaded *"Come ba-a-ack, Schoen!"* Most of the players had recently seen the movie, and they cracked up. Even Tom Blackburn couldn't suppress a smile.

During practice we automatically braced ourselves for Blackburn's deadly serious verbal attacks, but some of it was funny when my teammates and I kidded each other about it after practice. Few Flyer big men escaped one of Tom's favorite criticisms, delivered in his loud but controlled, derisive baritone voice "you are big enough to hunt bears with a switch, but you let that little guy take the rebound away from you."

In the first practice of my junior year I missed a jump shot Tom didn't like, and he sneered, "There's old Schoen, back again this year and the same old shot." Two of my teammates were from Cincinnati, and Tom often threatened to send one or the other of them "hitchhiking south on I-75." I soon lost count of how often he threatened to send me back to the farm if I didn't rebound harder or play with more intensity.

His attacks were hard to take sometimes, but misery loves company. As mid-1950s Flyer Jim Paxson once said in an interview, "Coach Blackburn treated us all the same – badly." He did not befriend any of his players and many were as intimidated by him as I was in my first two years. We found comfort in being unified against him in some ways, as when we made mock serious plans to attack him after practice someday soon. Our idea was a student manager would switch off the lights above the Fieldhouse floor just as Tom dismissed us at the end of practice. In the dark, we'd throw a large blanket or tarp over his head and all pounce on him, kicking and swinging. The attack never happened, of course, but joking about it was enough to relieve some of the tension his methods brought on.

Tough as it was to play for him, he was a successful coach who got good, disciplined effort from most of his players. He believed in a simple deliberate offense and a tough, usually man-to-man defense. Not one to substitute much, he thought there were five best players on any team, and his job was to find them and play them as much as possible. If you were not in his top five, or at most seven, you could expect to be on the bench only getting to play for a few minutes at the end of "blowout" games.

During games, Tom sat on the bench never getting up or seeming from a distance to be much into the game except at timeouts. People sometimes commented on how calm he was during games. In fact, when you sat next to him on the bench it was obvious he was anything but calm. He usually had a program in his hands that he twisted into a tight roll, then opened it and twisted it in the other direction, repeating again and again. Under his breath, he was criticizing, sometimes cursing, what his players were doing on the court.

* * *

As a sophomore, I was one of the team's benchwarmers. I got some positive attention in just one game, at home against Seton Hall just before Christmas. We started out poorly and were behind 13-7 when, to my complete surprise, Tom put me in early in the first half and played me for the rest of the game. After getting over some initial nervousness, I rebounded, scored and made two or three good passes in a run that put us ahead 18-13. I also played strong defense against their top scorer, and we won by an unexpectedly large 21-point margin.

After the game, sportswriters in the Dayton newspapers were favorably impressed with my play, and one of the papers ran my picture with a headline about me being a promising new addition to "Blackburn's stable of big men." I was expecting to get more playing time after that; the newspaper articles predicted as much but, for reasons he never revealed to me, Tom had other ideas. I saw no action in the next game, a ten-point loss against the powerful University of Cincinnati Bearcats, who went on to win the NCAA tournament that year and again the next. In fact, I never got another real opportunity in a game the rest of the season.

In spite of limited playing time and the constant pressure of trying to please Tom, I had many new and broadening experiences in my sophomore season. Because of their successes on the national stage in the 1950s, the UD Flyers basketball team was the toast of the town of Dayton. The UD Fieldhouse seated just short of 6,000 people, tickets were in short supply, and there was rarely an empty seat.

For thousands of people in Dayton, a night of Flyer basketball was one of the top social events in town. People dressed up for the games, frequently going out to dinner first. Because interest in the Flyers was high and Fieldhouse seating was limited, local television stations televised more and more home games each year, and some away games as well. By 1960, the Flyers had more regional television exposure than most other major college basketball teams. Besides the regional coverage, one or two games in my junior and senior years were televised nationally.

As a result, Flyers who played a lot were local celebrities, and the names of even the lowest benchwarmers like me were familiar to fans in the southwest region of Ohio covered by Dayton television. Kids asked for our autographs after games. Complete strangers came up, asked us questions about the team or the prospects for next year, and wished us well. We were desirable guests at parties, often getting invited not only to students' parties but also in groups to wealthy, or so they seemed at the time, Dayton people's homes for dinner.

Many UD students were Flyer fans, so players were well known on campus although some students resented the special treatment we received. All this attention was exhilarating, but at first it was awkward for me. Over time I became more comfortable in my role. I also did my best to stay focused on the reason I was at UD. I wanted to do as well as I could in basketball, but for me it was mainly the means to pay the bills for my college education.

Basketball at UD also provided me with opportunities for incidental learning off the court to an extent I hadn't expected. As a sophomore, I flew in an airplane for the first time. In fact, by the end of the season after about ten flights to away games, the workings of airports and the experience of flying had become commonplace. The most memorable trips for me were to New York City to play Seton Hall in February and for the NIT in March. We played these games in Madison Square Garden, the

Mecca of college basketball at the time.

Madison Square Garden used until 1968; on 8ᵗʰ Ave. between 49ᵗʰ & 50ᵗʰ Sts.

In our re-match against Seton Hall we scored 112 points, then the Garden record for the most points scored by a college team I played six or eight minutes, more than usual because of the lopsided score. Madison Square Garden was a huge impressive old place full of sports and entertainment tradition, but I was surprised the basketball floor was uneven and had dead spots as it was laid over hockey ice. The rims were "soft" allowing some shots to go in that may have bounced away on many courts.

I didn't get into any of the NIT games that year, but the team made it to the semifinals before losing. In my junior year, we played in two tournaments in Madison Square Garden, the Holiday Festival at Christmas time and the NIT. In my senior year, we played Providence there at the end of January.

Beyond the thrill of playing basketball in Madison Square Garden, those New York City trips were educational for a young person with a background like mine. For several days while the tournaments were in progress and for two days for single games, we stayed in a nice hotel just off Broadway, the Hotel Picadilly on 45ᵗʰ Street. We ate our meals in good, but usually not fancy, restaurants. Sometimes we were allowed to order off the menu ourselves, another new experience for me.

On some days when we had no game, athletic director Harry Baujan arranged for us to attend a Broadway play in the evening. During my three years on the Flyer varsity, I remember seeing *Bye Bye Birdie*, *Something's Got to Give* and *West Side Story*. I passed up a chance to see Broadway legend Mary Martin in *Sound of Music* as a guest of teammate Don (Goose) Heller's parents, and I've kicked myself for that ever since.

One evening, some friends and I walked several blocks from the Picadilly to the Peppermint Lounge, where the era's most popular dance, the twist, originated. The place was too packed for us to get in, but we stood on the sidewalk for a while and watched Chubby Checker performing the twist as he sang "Come on baby, let's do the twist."

* * *

Throughout my years at UD, I was a consistent B+ to A student. I was most comfortable and successful in my math classes, but I did at least B+ work in all areas of study. My two one-semester freshman math courses, College Algebra and Trigonometry, were largely repeats of content I had in high school, and I did well in Calculus I and II in my sophomore year. On the whole I enjoyed my UD class work though, of course, some classes and some professors were more interesting than others.

All students were required to take either a philosophy or a religion class each semester, and I enjoyed my introductions to areas of philosophy. It was completely new to me to think and reason about various facets of the human experience and to study about the great thinkers of history.

I also liked the relatively open-ended nature of some professors' assignments, as this allowed me to pursue some of my own interests. For example, I wrote a research paper for a freshman English class on the 1919 Chicago Black Sox scandal that was one of the most enjoyable class assignments I ever had.

My study time was limited by basketball during the season, and the dormitory atmosphere was not favorable for studying. But I had learned efficient study habits in high school including how to focus my attention on key course material and block out background noise. To avoid the dormitory chaos, I usually studied in the library. Knowing I'd have some busy times when basketball distracted me, I did my best to stay current in my courses at all times and never to procrastinate on long-term assignments.

The most natural friendships for me at UD were with my teammates since we had many shared goals and experiences. The development of these friendships was delayed because I lived in a different dormitory than the other freshman players. Once freshman practices started I got to know the other guys, who all called me Harry. A group of us often had dinner in the cafeteria after practice, and they began to invite me to join them in their weekend social activities. I usually had fun, and it always felt comfortable to be around a group of guys in which I was not six inches taller than anyone else.

My teammates were a mixed group, many from small towns in Ohio and some from cities like Cincinnati, Detroit, Cleveland, Chicago, and Columbus. In my junior and senior years, a teammate was from New York City and another from Philadelphia. I was the only Flyer basketball player in my four years who grew up on a farm. I respected the basketball talents of all my teammates and I liked most of them personally, but just two became good, life-long friends.

Bill Westerkamp from Cincinnati was our class's 6'10" center. Bill was outgoing and had an off-beat, satirical sense of humor I found really funny. He also went out of his way more than anyone else on the team to include me in social activities during freshman year, and I appreciated that. Paul Winterhalter from Tiffin, a guard, was the leading scorer in the state of Ohio as a high school senior. Paul was a serious political science student on his way to becoming a successful lawyer, a profession he still practices in Dayton. Paul was the only one of my teammates who studied more than I did, and we studied together most weeknights in the Library.

Paul (33), Bill (21) in action

Making new friends helped but as a homesick freshman, I still went home every chance I could. When I visited home back then, I felt tremendous relief and comfort to be in the setting that was so familiar to me. I was able to put the stress and tension of being in Dayton, living in the dorm, and dealing with basketball pressures aside for a while.

On those short visits, I mainly stayed home and enjoyed activities with the family. One weekend night when I was at home, Jim and I took Rick who was only about ten or eleven at the time to Portland to see a horror film double feature. One of the movies was *House on the Haunted Hill* starring Vincent Price. I don't remember the name of the other feature, but the night stands out in my mind because it is my only memory of just the three of us having an evening out.

After basketball practices began, I wasn't able to go home on weekends but freshman players were allowed one or two days off at Thanksgiving and about a week at Christmas. During freshman year, I began to adjust to being away from home for long periods, but I never stopped enjoying getting home.

In 1960; Seated l to r: Linda, Doris. Standing 1st row: Rick, Marilyn, Dan, Dave; 2nd row: Pat, Janice, Eileen, Ginny, Mom, Dad, Kate. Back row, Jim, me

* * *

In the summer following freshman year, I lived at home and worked full-time at the Equity Dairy in Fort Recovery. I worked from 5:00 pm until after midnight, and each week I was scheduled to work five of the seven nights. The two nights I didn't work varied from week to week, and they were not necessarily consecutive. Since my friends were on regular daytime work schedules, my irregular schedule made for a socially boring and lonesome summer. I even had to leave Sunday afternoon softball games early if I worked that night.

As often as I could, I played pick-up basketball games on an outdoor court at the Coldwater Park with several college players home for the summer. Some area high school stars played, too, including my former FRHS teammate Dave Williams, who as a junior was one of the top scorers in the MCL, and Jim who was a regular on the FRHS varsity the previous year as a freshman.

In June that summer, Bob Fiely asked me to coach Fort Recovery's entry in the new Mercer County Babe Ruth Baseball League for 13-15 year-olds, a group that included Jim. The idea of coaching my brother appealed to me, and I needed to amass some hours working with young people for my teacher preparation program at UD, so I agreed. At 19, it was easy for me to identify with the players who were only four or five years younger. We had a good team finishing near the top of the league, but neither Jim nor I can remember whether we had the best record in the league.

Jim was by far the top pitcher and we had a good catcher, Jim's classmate Dan Eifert. When they were our pitcher and catcher, we were competitive against anyone in the league. Jim pitched a no-hitter in a game in which the opposing pitcher did, too, but because of errors, walks, and passed balls on both sides we won 2-1.

In a game Dan had to miss, our second pitcher and catcher were having lots of problems, but we were hitting well and had a lead when I put Jim in to pitch the last inning. He faced four batters, struck out all of them, yet the other team scored a run because our second-string catcher couldn't handle many of Jim's pitches. At the end of the season, each team was given two slots on a league all-star team, and I did not hesitate to nominate Jim and Dan as our all-stars. The season was a lot of fun and convinced me I'd enjoy being a coach.

Overall though, the summer had been pretty lonesome and boring for me, and I was glad to get back to UD when classes started. That was my last summer at home as I took a job in Dayton at Inland Manufacturing after my sophomore year. Ed Kemper invited me to move into a house he and his brother Dick were sharing with a friend of Dick's. With Dick's financial backing, Ed was operating a one-man overhead garage door company, The Metropolitan Door Company or as we affectionately called it, "The Met". That year and the next two, I had pleasant and interesting summers working in Dayton, living with the Kempers during the week, and riding home with them on weekends.

Looking back at my first two years at UD, I was feeling OK. I was successful in my studies. In basketball, I had survived a difficult freshman adjustment and, with several breaks along the way, made the varsity as a sophomore. I sat on the bench all sophomore year, but I had many new experiences to make up for that disappointment. Little did I suspect what was in store for me in the next basketball season.

8 A SEASON TO REMEMBER

At the end of the 1960-61 season the Flyers and their fans were excited about next year. Two of our best players, forward Garry Roggenburk and guard Tommy Hatton, were back for their senior year, and they'd be joined by members of a freshman team that won 36 games and lost only four. The freshmen were led by two former high school All-Americans, 6'4" forward Roger Brown and 6'10" center Bill Chmielewski, and their top guard was Gordie Hatton, Tommy's younger brother. Most people were predicting next year's team would be a truly great college team, and I thought so, too. I didn't expect to play much with such a talented group of teammates, but it'd be fun to have even a small role on a great team.

Roger was a tremendous player. He was a great shooter; in his first freshman game, he hit 13 of 13 shots from the field. But he was outstanding in all phases of the game. He was an incredible passer and could jump as well as anyone I ever played with or against. His one-on-one moves were smooth and quick, and he seemed always in complete control of his body.

I remember guarding him in varsity versus freshman scrimmages, which were always close and sometimes won by the freshman team. Once he went up for a jump shot against me, and

I was right up on him. He shot the ball with his right hand and pushed my hands away with his left. I said, "That's a foul, Roger." He smiled and replied, "Yeah, but they'd call it on you."

In spring of 1961 after the season was over Roger, who was from Brooklyn, was granted immunity to testify against some New York City gamblers he had met as a high school senior. The gamblers were being indicted for paying college players to shave points in the last two or three seasons. During the trial, several college players admitted to shaving points to make some of their team's losses beat the point spread for the gamblers.

Two of them were the two top scorers from Seton Hall, and one game in which they were paid was against us in February 1961 when we set the Madison Square Garden single college game scoring record. In that game, I guarded one of the point shavers for a while. He mostly stood around in the corner on offense, but at the time I just assumed I was playing good defense and he was having a down game. The thought never occurred to me that he was deliberately playing poorly.

I read that the Seton Hall coach and teammates of the two point shavers had a similar reaction. They should have known something shady was going on, but it never occurred to them their own players or teammates would do such a thing. Seeing this phenomenon up close, I understood better why the 1919 Black Sox and the 1951 college basketball scandals were not immediately detected and exposed.

No charges were filed against Roger, but nevertheless he was barred for life from college basketball and from the NBA. It was assumed the gamblers intended to engage him in point shaving after he became a varsity player. My teammates and I were devastated as we considered Roger to be not only one of the best players we had ever seen but also a nice guy. UD fans' excitement for the team's prospects was replaced by curiosity about how Coach Blackburn and the remaining, still pretty talented, group of players would cope with the loss of Roger.

* * *

Whatever was in Blackburn's mind about the team at the beginning of practice in mid-October 1961, I did not have a prominent place in his thinking as is clear in this team picture taken on the first day of practice. For the picture, Tom placed the players who were likely starters or early substitutes in the first row, and those destined to be benchwarmers in the back row where my presence is prominent.

1961-62; first row, l to r: manager Tony Scalia, Ron Anello, Bill Westerkamp, Tommy Hatton, Garry Roggenburk, Bill Chmielewski. Gordie Hatton, Stan Greenberg; 2nd row, Coach Tom Blackburn, Jimmie Powers, Dan Mueller, me, Chuck Izor, Paul Winterhalter, Don Smith, athletic director Harry Baujan

Compared to my sophomore year when he yelled at me constantly, this year he paid little attention to me in practice. It was a relief in a way, but it meant he had at least temporarily given up on me.

As the season drew near, four players had locks on starting positions, the Hatton brothers, Roggenburk and Chmielewski. In early games, Blackburn played a "big" line-up with Bill Westerkamp as the fifth starter. With this team on the court, Westerkamp played center and Chim moved to forward even

161

though both were used to playing center. A problem for the two centers was one of them had to guard a forward, and neither was used to guarding a man who was facing the basket. Quick forwards gave them fits. We won our first six games so Tom stuck mainly with this group.

When the big lineup was having difficulties, Tom switched to a "small" lineup with senior 6'1" guard Stan Greenberg replacing Westerkamp. Chim moved to center and Greenberg played as a third guard or small forward. This lineup was quicker than the big lineup, but Greenberg or Gordie Hatton had to guard a forward who may be five or six inches taller. Of course, Roggenburk guarded one forward but he was an outstanding offensive player, and it would be a mistake to make him concentrate too hard on defense. As the competition began to get tougher after Christmas (or as Tom liked to warn us each year at Christmas time, "The bears are just around the corner"), the weaknesses of these combinations became more and more problematic.

We lost for the first time in the Holiday Festival in New York to a good Wisconsin team, and then won two more before an unexpected ten-point loss to Canisius followed by a devastating 20-point loss to eighth ranked Duquesne in Pittsburgh. After the Duquesne game, a group of UD students hung Tom in effigy, treatment he was not used to and did not like at all. He was quoted in the newspaper at the time as saying, "We are just not a very good team."

We came back with a close home court win against Louisville, in spite of over 30 points by the UL center mainly on quick moves around the basket. Then we were trounced by 1961 and soon to be 1962 NCAA champion, the University of Cincinnati. Tom played my classmate 6'6" Ron Anello at forward opposite Roggenburk in one or two of these games, but Ron was a natural center both offensively and defensively so he did not solve the problems the other big lineup was having.

162

During this time, I continued to warm the bench as I had all season and most of the previous one. Worse, my UD career had reached its low point on the night of our game at Canisius when I hid in embarrassment in my dorm room so as few people as possible would notice I was the only Flyer not on the traveling squad.

* * *

Tommy Hatton, who was the team's co-captain with Garry, told me later that after the Cincinnati loss Blackburn asked him, "Well, what do we do now?" Tommy replied, "Try Schoen." And he did. We were scheduled to play a pretty good Eastern Kentucky team several days after the UC loss, and Blackburn told me I would start and guard their top scorer, a forward averaging 22 points per game.

Don Donoher, a former Flyer player, was Tom's top scout, and he worked with me in practice on how to defend against my man. Rather than follow the usual rule at the time that a defensive man should always stay between his man and the basket in order to be in position to guard him when he got the ball, I was to stay between my man and the ball so my man could not get the ball. This approach to defense is standard today but was unusual in 1962.

At 4:00 pm on the day of each home game, the team had a pre-game meal in the Chaminade Hall cafeteria. Before every game, we had the same menu that was different from what athletes these days eat. The belief was a high protein meal provided the most energy by game time, four hours later, so we had steak, baked potato, a cooked vegetable, and toast with honey.

Tom, athletic director Harry Baujan, and trainer Eddie Kwest had dinner with the team arriving and leaving together in Baujan's car. After this team meal, Tom changed his routine and walked by himself from Chaminade Hall down the hill to the Fieldhouse in the hope this change of routine would result in an improvement in the team's fortunes. This game was clearly important to our superstitious coach.

I was nervous going into the game, but also determined not to mess up this opportunity. The man I was guarding played in the corner where he was a good shot, but he didn't move quickly without the ball. Donoher's work with me in practice had been right on target. I overplayed him when the ball came to his side of the court, so his teammate at guard rarely got the ball to him. He scored just six points while I had 14 points and 10 rebounds. We won 97-66.

I started and we won the next two games. The first was a big double overtime win at DePaul, coached by Tom's friend and rival, Ray Meyer, the great George Mikan's college coach in the 1940s. With six or eight seconds to go in the second overtime, the score was tied and we had the ball on their end of the court. We called timeout. The excitement in the DePaul arena was intense, and Blackburn was frantic. As I recall, he asked anxiously, "What should we do? You guys are out there on the court. What do you think will work?" The question was mainly addressed to our senior co-captains.

To his credit as a team leader, Tommy had a great idea. The play he designed had Garry take the ball out of bounds. Tommy, our fastest guard, lined up about midcourt on the right side with the other guard in a similar position on the left side. Bill Westerkamp and I stayed on our end of the court but on the left side so there was a big opening at our end on the right side. When the ref handed Garry the ball, Tommy faked coming forward to get it, then took off at top speed past his defensive man along the right side of the court toward our basket.

Garry whipped the ball as only he could at least three-fourths the length of the court to Tommy who took a dribble or two and pulled up about 15 feet from the basket as if to shoot a jump shot. By this time, Bill's man had run over to try to stop Tommy. Spotting Bill wide open underneath, Tommy lobbed the ball using his jump shot motion to Bill who jumped high, grabbed it with two hands and dropped it in for the win.

The next game, a five-point win at home against a strong Drake team coached by Maury John, was my best offensive game of the year. I scored 19 points on seven of nine from the field and five of five free throws, four of which were crucial in the last two minutes of the game. I also held the high scoring Drake center to eight points. The team was 3-0 in my first three starts, I had scored 42 points and my defensive assignments, always one of the top scorers on the opposing team, had scored a total of 18 points. I was feeling great about then, thinking I was finally making important contributions to the team's success, but without warning things turned sour.

We had a tough one-point loss at Xavier, a game we should have won. Tom was not pleased with some of my shot selection. Xavier played a solid man-to-man defense, and I think my recent high scoring games prompted me to force a few shots. As I soon realized, my highest scoring games usually came against a zone defense. I did not have great offensive moves to consistently shake loose from a good defensive man, but against a zone I played the high post (around the free-throw line). As the team passed the ball rapidly around the court I sometimes got fairly open jump shots from 15 to 18 feet, and I was deadly with those.

I learned some realism about my offensive skills against Xavier, and the next game provided a difficult lesson about the limits of my defensive skills. The University of Detroit came to Dayton with their senior first team all-American, 6'6" Dave DeBusschere. He was one of the two or three top college players in the country averaging over 25 points and about 20 rebounds, among the top ten or so in both categories. He was a tremendous all-around athlete, capable of playing superbly anywhere on the basketball court. For a couple of years after college, he starred in the NBA and pitched regularly for the Chicago White Sox before he decided to focus on basketball. In his NBA career, he was best known as one of the key members of the fabulous New York Knicks teams of the late 1960s and early 1970s.

I am trying to be as complimentary of DeBusschere as I can, because I have no excuse for how completely he dominated me that night. He had played an inside game when our scout saw him play, so I prepared to fight him hard for position inside in order to make it difficult for him to get the ball. That was in practice. In the game, on Detroit's first possession DeBusschere came dribbling down the court, pulled up and swished a 25-foot jump shot. The next time the same, then a fake and a drive in for a lay-up. Then more long jump shots, hardly ever missing.

Trying to pressure his shots, I fouled him three times in the first ten minutes. Tom took me out and tried some of my teammates on him and then me again later, but nobody could stop him that night. He scored 44 points, the most by a visiting player in the history of the UD Fieldhouse, and we lost by 22. I was scoreless and demoralized. Immediately after the game, our furious coach told us to get into our practice clothes, and he put us through an hour or two of practice including some punishing running drills before allowing us to limp off to bed.

Everyone including Tom was depressed in practices before the next game against the University of Portland at home. Tom was still using me as a possible starter in practice, so I didn't think the Detroit game had completely soured him on me. However, after five straight starts, I was on the bench to begin the game. Dad told me later, Coach Blackburn in his pre-game remarks on the radio said I was not starting as I "was still recovering from the Detroit game."

I wondered briefly if I would be banished back to the bench full-time, but within four or five minutes we fell behind and Tom put me in. I think it was a smart move on his part not to start me, because when I got the call I felt a surge of energy. I played extra hard to avoid going back to my benchwarmer role. I didn't score more than a few points but played good defense, and we won by three. This game got me back into the starting lineup where I stayed through my senior year.

After the Portland game Tom told me, "Don't worry about scoring. These other guys can score. You just concentrate on stopping the man you're guarding." I was to be the defensive ace of the team and always guard the top scorer unless he was a little guard. I took Tom seriously and began to focus on keeping my man from scoring.

When we were on offense, I continued to watch where my man was so as soon as the ball changed hands I could rush to keep pressure on him and never let him get an easy basket. I became pretty good at overplaying players so they had a hard time getting the ball. Based on Don Donoher's scouting reports, I prepared in practice for the strengths and weaknesses of the player I was assigned to guard and for where he was likely to go on the court to get the ball so I could beat him to the spot. On offense, I mainly fed the ball to our center as Blackburn's offensive plays called for. I didn't completely stop scoring after that, but I had no more 19-point games until my senior year.

The team caught fire then winning our last six season games by an average margin of 16 points. Everyone was playing well most of the time. If a starter had foul trouble or a bad game Greenberg or Westerkamp came in and took up the slack. The other four starters provided well-balanced scoring, each averaging 11 to 16 points per game for the season. I contributed another 8 or 9 points and pretty consistently shut down, or at least kept in check, the opposing teams' top scoring forward or center. In that stretch, two games stand out as our most important wins and I believe the ones Coach Blackburn savored most.

The first game after Portland was a re-match at home with Duquesne who had beaten us by 20 points earlier in the year and was still ranked in the top ten in the country. I don't think Tom had gotten over being hung in effigy after that game. He also disliked their coach, Red Manning, whose teams had a reputation for getting into brawls with their opponents.

Chim (15), Garry (43), and Gordie (12) watch my rebound vs Duquesne.

When we began to prepare for Duquesne in practice, Tom urged us not to be intimidated by any of their players. "If they start pushing you around, push back." He went on to assure us "if Manning tries anything, I'll take care of him."

We had never heard him say anything like that about an opposing coach before, and it may have helped fire us up. The man I guarded was one of the players who had a particularly shady reputation, but there were no problems in this game. We completely dominated them for the entire game, winning 71-48.

Our closest game in this stretch was a six-point win at Louisville. UD and UL had a great rivalry in which most years UD won at home and UL won in their arena. Tom had a lot of respect for their coach, Peck Hickman, so he loved to beat UL in Louisville. In contrast to the UD Fieldhouse, Louisville played in a huge arena, Freedom Hall, that could seat about 19,000 people for basketball.

I was assigned to guard their center who had scored over 30 points against us in Dayton when I was a bench warmer. He scored most of his points in that game on a play that involved one or two picks and ended with him getting a pass low on the right side of the basket, turning quickly to his left and driving along the baseline for a layup.

In practice, we developed a plan to defend against this play. When the play began, instead of following my man through the picks, I ran straight to the spot on the right side of the basket where he would end up. I stayed in front of him to deny him the pass, and if he was on the verge of getting the ball I jumped quickly to the baseline behind him because he always turned that way. That play rarely worked for them all night, so I was a little surprised when with 20 or 30 seconds to go and behind by two points, they chose to try to tie the game with the same play.

I pressured their center into missing an off-balance shot, and Garry got the rebound. I raced down to our end of the court in time to get fouled as I rebounded a teammate's missed shot. I made both free throws to put us up by four, and a steal and basket by Tommy Hatton iced the game. Tom ignored me in the locker room after the game, but to the sportswriters he said, "Wasn't Schoen great?" He also declared after this win we deserved to be in the top ten teams in the country, although we never officially had that distinction during the season.

Our season had been like three different seasons: the first six games, the next 13, and the last seven. Playing mainly our big lineup, we won the first six games although the opposing teams were not as strong as they became after that. The next 13 games were transitional as the weaknesses of Blackburn's big and little lineups became increasingly apparent, and then we all began to adjust to our new starting lineup. We were inconsistent with a 7-6 record during that stretch. Finally we put everything together as a team and began to play consistently well, winning our last seven games usually by wide margins. We ended the season at 20-6 and accepted our invitation to the NIT.

* * *

Of the twelve teams who were to play in the NIT, the four the tournament organizers considered the best were seeded and given a bye in the first round. In spite of our seven-game winning streak and 20 wins, we were not seeded, so we played on the first night of the tournament, Thursday, March 13. If we continued to win, we played again on Saturday, then the following Thursday, and in the final game on Saturday, March 22.

One logistical issue Baujan and Blackburn needed to work out was whether to stay in New York for the four days between the second and third games, or return to Dayton so we could attend classes. As I recall, Tom definitely favored staying so we could better keep our minds on the task at hand, winning the NIT. After some discussion, the decision was to stay in New York at the Hotel Picadilly for the entire 10 days. This meant a player in a class that met on Monday, Wednesday, and Friday as many did, missed five consecutive classes.

It would be difficult to keep up especially in my Differential Equations class. Before we left for New York, I went to talk to the professor who gave me some problems and text assignments I could work at on my own on the trip. He also gave me the name and phone number of a highly qualified mathematics teacher at Chaminade High School in Brooklyn in case I needed help. I told him I'd try to keep up, but the basketball demands will make it tough to concentrate on studying.

My studies had already suffered a little since I began to play regularly. I still kept my regular study schedule with Paul Winterhalter, but it was often hard for me to concentrate on the class work. I was always nervous on game days. It was hard to turn off the adrenalin and get to sleep the night after a game, and the next day I usually felt drained physically and emotionally. I had a small taste of such ups and downs in high school basketball, but at UD they were more intense. In the days leading up to the NIT and during the tournament, the intensity peaked. Off the court during the tournament, I never calmed down completely.

The team had been playing so well in the last month the players were cautiously optimistic about our chances in the NIT. Our coach, though, was very nervous about our first game against Wichita. A member of the strong Missouri Valley Conference, they had won two of three games against Big Ten teams early in the year. They also split with other MVC powers Bradley, Drake, and NCAA champion UC. Their record was only 18-8, but they obviously had a demanding schedule. All-American forward 6'7" Dave Stallworth and 6'11" center Gene Wiley were their top players. They were well-coached by a young Ralph Miller, who went on to a long and distinguished coaching career at the University of Iowa and Oregon State.

Stallworth was a good player, too quick for me to keep from getting the ball consistently and an excellent shot. I worked hard against him, but he scored 18 points, which was still six below his season average. Garry and Tommy played their usual top-notch basketball as they did throughout the tournament, but our two sophomores, Chim and Gordie, had exceptional games. Chim scored 24 and completely outplayed Wiley, and Gordie was second high on the team with 19. We beat Wichita 79-71.

After that win, I felt pretty confident we could win the tournament. We were already a good team at the end of the season, and the way Chim and Gordie were playing I didn't see how anyone could beat us. Our quarterfinal game on Saturday was against Houston, seeded with a 21-5 record. It was no contest as Chim and Gordie scored 32 and 24, respectively. I guarded their top scorer who had averaged about 16 points per game during the season. He was a good shooter but not quick. I overplayed him to keep the ball out of his hands, and he did not score all night. We won by 17 points but were ahead at one time by 29.

The semifinal games were on Thursday night, so we had four days to wait. Tom tried to schedule practice time for us every day in the Garden, but a Rangers hockey game was scheduled for

Tuesday night so the basketball floor was not available for us. Tom or Harry Baujan arranged a practice time at nearby Power Memorial Academy. When we walked into the school gym, the junior high team was finishing their practice.

Our attention went immediately to a tall (maybe 6'6"), skinny kid, who was not only head and shoulders above the other kids in height but was clearly a gifted athlete. His name was Lew Alcindor, later to star at UCLA on three great national championship teams and in the NBA as Kareem Abdul-Jabbar. In eighth grade, he was already getting lots of national attention, as evidenced by the fact sitting in the bleachers watching this junior high team practice were Coach Red Auerbach and star center Bill Russell of the Boston Celtics who were in town to play the New York Knicks the next night.

Usually on road trips, we ate our meals, at least lunch and dinner, together as a team. With four days between games, Tom decided we could eat lunch on our own in the Picadilly's lobby café and bill it to our rooms. At first, he said we could order any sandwich on the menu. He was thinking of a hamburger or ham & cheese, but we soon discovered they had a sirloin steak sandwich. It was a nice cut of sirloin served between two pieces of toast, and it was priced like a steak at $7 or $8 while a hamburger was $1.50 or $2.

For a day or two, everyone ordered the sirloin sandwich until Harry Baujan saw the bills. He gave us a lecture about how much this was costing and assured us when we got out of school and had to pay the bills on trips ourselves, we'd be more frugal. Tom agreed half-heartedly with Harry and we were no longer allowed to order the sirloin sandwich for lunch, but we were about to win the NIT so they were pretty nice to us.

Meanwhile, back in Dayton, the students and fans were getting excited. Many students were from the East, so they could work out a reasonably inexpensive plan to attend our semifinal game, and hopefully the final one. Dayton tour companies

172

arranged trips, as did lots of fans privately. Unlike the first two games when we had little fan support, UD fans were well represented in the semifinal and final game crowds. They were also visible at the many victory parties after the final game.

Loyola of Chicago, our semifinal opponent, had a 22-3 record. All American forward 6'3" Jerry Harkness averaged 22 points per game during the season, and he'd be challenging to guard. In this game, we started slowly and were behind by three points at half time. I was struggling with Harkness who had ten points at the half. We re-grouped at half time and came out determined not to let this game get away.

Early in the second half Tommy Hatton sparked a 10-2 run with a steal and two quick baskets and we were ahead to stay. Gordie scored 33 points and, after a slow start, Chim had 27. I was the only starter not in double figures, scoring six with 11 rebounds. I did a much better job on Harkness in the second half, as he scored no more field goals and just two free throws. He was too quick for me to deny him the ball, but being four inches taller, I was able to block one or two of his shots and bother him badly on some others. We scored 57 points in the second half and won going away, 98-82.

My defense had been good in the first three games of the NIT, but I was less involved in the offense than I had been during the season, averaging just seven points per game. With Chim and Gordie doing so well, I mainly tried not to bog the offense down usually getting the ball to Chim or to another teammate, but rarely looking for a shot myself. Before the final game against St. John's, Tommy Hatton told me privately I should pick up my offensive game. I told him about Blackburn's expectations for me, but he said the team needed for me to look for a shot a little more often.

The final game was scheduled for national television at 4:00 pm on Saturday March 22 1962, the first game of a college basketball doubleheader. The second game was the 1962 NCAA

Tournament finals in which the University of Cincinnati beat Ohio State for the second straight year. St. John's had topped Duquesne by ten points in their semifinal NIT game to bring their record to 23-5. Madison Square Garden was practically a home court for St. John's, as they played many season games there. They also had won three NIT championships in 13 previous tournament appearances, so this was not a new experience for them.

I was still confident we'd win but was awestruck to be in this position. On Friday March 21 I wrote a long letter to Jim trying to tell him about my feelings of nervousness and awe, yet confidence in the team. I don't remember exactly what I wrote, but I no doubt emphasized the contrast between basketball in the barn and in the Garden.

St. John's had three outstanding players, center Leroy Ellis, forward Willie Hall, and guard Kevin Loughery. Having seen them play in the semifinal game, I expected to guard Hall but Tom put me on 6'3" Loughery. He was a great shooter and considerably quicker than I was. Loughery went on to a productive NBA career as a player and coach. He had the distinction of coaching two young greats in the 1970s, Julius Erving (Dr. J) in the ABA for two years and Michael Jordan in his rookie year as a Chicago Bull.

On one of our early possessions in the game, I hit a one-handed set shot from the corner. After missing a second one a little later, Tommy Hatton whispered, "Don't get carried away." I continued to take shots as they came up and was five of six from the field by half time. On one of my baskets we took the lead for good with four minutes to play in the first half. They stayed close, getting to within three points once or twice but when they did we always rallied, winning the game 73-67. Once again, Chim was the big hero with 24 points and 11 rebounds, and Gordie added 18 points. I scored 12 points, but Loughery gave me fits, drawing me into fouls and scoring 24 points. With a couple of minutes to go in the game I fouled out, my first time as a Flyer.

I felt bad about fouling out, but the game was under control and sitting on the bench beside Tom as he was on the verge of realizing his elusive dream was interesting. He was incredibly nervous at first, criticizing under his breath his team's performance on the court. With a little under a minute left, St. John's coach Joe Lapchick walked over and shook Tom's hand, congratulating him on his first NIT win in ten tries. Tom smiled broadly and began to relax.

Chim, Garry, Coach, Tommy, me, Gordie. Picture covers a wall in the UD Arena lobby.

As the final minute wound down, Flyer fans were getting louder and more excited by the second. As a fan myself since 1953, I appreciated the significance of this moment in the history of UD basketball and was happy to be part of it. As the game ended, I turned toward Tom intending to congratulate him but he had already turned away to shake hands with his friend, team doctor George Rau, and celebrate with him. I was left to seek out some of my teammates so we could jump for joy together and help each other fend off the horde of well-meaning fans pummeling us.

The bedlam on the court lasted a long time, but finally the floor was cleared for the closing ceremonies. Tom grinned from ear to ear when he went up to receive the championship trophy, saying, "It's been a long time coming and I'm going to hang on to it and enjoy it as long as I can." Chim was the most valuable player and Gordie was named to the all-tournament team, both well-deserved honors. They were good all season, but in the NIT – Wow! Chim averaged over 26 points per game, and Gordie over 23; both stats were more than ten points per game above their season averages.

St. John's coach Lapchick was impressed with Chim, predicting "The big guy will make Dayton the Ohio State of next year, and he will be the next Jerry Lucas [Ohio State's superstar senior center]. He's one of the best young big men I've seen come along."

As reported in the media, Tom was complimentary of all his players including me. He said I played great defense during the tournament, and even when Loughery proved to be too quick I kept working and never gave up on him. In *Sports Illustrated* April 2 1962, he is quoted as saying we were "The best team I've ever had", a complete reversal of his early January assessment, "We are just not a very good team."

The best compliment I was paid was by All-American Jerry Harkness a year later. In 1963, senior Harkness led Loyola to the NCAA championship. A *Dayton Journal Herald* sportswriter interviewed him before the NCAA semifinal games, today called the Final Four. Harkness grew up in Harlem where he played against Roger Brown who he said was a great player. He also recalled Loyola's loss to us in the 1962 NIT and said "That guy [Schoen] held me down real good. What a defensive player he was against us. When I did manage to get away from him and go inside, then there was that big Chmielewski waiting for me."

Tom and team's triumphant return to Dayton; reception at the Fieldhouse

I performed my defensive role well, but I was the "unsung Schoen" or as one reporter wrote "the unheralded Schoen." Big scorers always get the most media attention, but I was no doubt the fifth best player of the starters. All four of my teammates are either in UD's Basketball Hall of Fame and/or on its All-Twentieth Century Team. Garry Roggenburk and Bill Chmielewski were All-Americans in 1962. Garry was inducted into the Ohio Basketball Hall of Fame in 2014, seven years after the 1961-62 Flyers were installed as a team.

I was fortunate to be on a team with such a talented group of players. I am proud to have been a member of the team and to be able to say the team played better when I was in the game. One of my few disappointments about the season is no one had the opportunity to see how good the Flyers would have been if Roger Brown had played.

Back home, my parents and younger siblings were glued to the family's fuzzy, black-and-white 19-inch t.v. for all the NIT games. Pat recalled, "After the final game we went outside and ran around the house yelling and screaming. It was a thrill for all of us. What a great memory!"

When the team returned on Sunday March 23rd, Mom, Dad, and a carload of siblings were in the crowd at the Dayton airport. After ten days in New York City competing in Madison Square Garden, I was struck the moment I saw them by the vast difference between the world I just left and that of my childhood.

With the NIT victory accomplished, I was anxious to get back to being a college student, but that would not be easy.

9 STUDENT LIFE

Basketball wasn't my entire life at UD, although it sometimes seemed to be. From the opening of fall semester near the end of September, it was just a few weeks until official practice began on October 15. From then until the season ended in March, late March in years we went to the NIT, life for me as a UD student was dominated by basketball and keeping up in my classes. The remaining six or eight weeks of classes in the Spring was the only time I had to be anything like a normal college student.

This "normal" life completely eluded me in the Spring of 1962 following our NIT victory. From our return to Dayton to a huge reception in the Fieldhouse the day after the final game until the semester ended in mid-May, we were swamped with invitations to testimonials, dinners, and parties in our honor. Along with the UC and OSU teams, the governor named us Honorary Attorney Generals of the State of Ohio. It was the best year ever for college basketball in Ohio. No Ohio college team has won the NCAA tournament since OSU won in 1960 and UC beat OSU in the final game in both 1961 and 1962.

I was invited to the FRHS athletic banquet to receive a nice trophy engraved "Congratulations Hal on the 1962 NIT. From your loyal fans in Fort Recovery." I was pleased to be at the

banquet, as Jim had just finished his junior year as a star pitcher and top scorer on the basketball team at 20-plus per game. Because of the Flyers schedule, I had never seen Jim play basketball in high school although I attended one game in his senior year.

I also had a great time playing in a charity basketball game on a FRHS alumni team with ex-teammate Dave Williams who was near the end of his freshman year as a basketball player at Findlay College. We eked out a victory over a good faculty team that included Bob Fiely, Jerry Brown, and Doc Knapke. To top off the nostalgic atmosphere of the game, one of the referees was an old rival of mine in basketball and baseball from St. Henry.

As a senior, Jim was the top player in the MCL and earned all-Ohio honorable mention.

Tommy Hatton and I gave one or two talks together at high school athletic banquets in the area that spring. I remember opening my talks with a couple of Yogi-isms (like "when you come to a fork in the road, take it" or "no one eats at this restaurant anymore; it's too crowded") from Yogi Berra who was nearing the end of his hall-of-fame career with the Yankees at the time. I am reminded of that because Yogi just died at 90 years of age a few days before I am writing these words.

At Dad's youngest sister Sally's invitation, Tommy and I also were special guests for lunch at a school for children with disabilities where she worked. We were both touched by how warm and open the kids were and what a thrill it was for them to be talking to us. All these invitations and honors were flattering, but they didn't help my performance in my classes. I was getting

180

more Bs and fewer As when compared to my first several semesters.

* * *

I have a certificate signed by UD president Raymond A. Roesch S.M. that verifies I "was one of the seventy-three men to live in famed St. Joseph Hall during the school year 1962 – 1963, the seventy-eighth and last year that venerable and honored edifice was used as a Student Residence Hall." That year was my fourth in St. Joe Hall, as we called it. UD varsity basketball players and football players roomed there along with a few other male students. My roommate as a junior and senior was classmate Dan Mueller, a guard from Delphos, Ohio, in the next county north of Mercer County. We had a lot in common and got along well. Bill and Paul roomed together just down the hall from us.

The dorm atmosphere was often chaotic and always lacking in privacy, but there were some good times. With so many guys interested in sports from different areas of the country, someone in the dorm was a fan of almost any major league baseball, basketball, and football team in the country. The conflicts between fans when their teams played against each other were interesting and often funny. Sports fans are just not objective about their teams, so the arguments about whose star was better, what strategies might win for each team, and who had the best manager or coach were endless and impossible to resolve.

A good example was the 1960 World Series between the Pittsburgh Pirates and New York Yankees. As usual in those years, the powerful Yankees were favored. Among the St. Joe residents, there were many Pirate fans and a smaller number of Yankee fans. They were going at each other from the Series' start to its finish. An unusual pattern of game scores helped to feed the verbal disputes between the fans.

The Pirates won the first game 6-4; then the Yankees crushed the Pirates in the next two games 16-3 and 10-0. At that point Yankee fans were cocky, and the Pittsburghers were despondent, nearly ready to throw in the towel. Surprisingly, the Pirates won the next two games 3-2 and 5-2, and it was their fans' turn to be cocky, but only briefly as the Yankees evened the series with another blowout 12-0.

The seventh game could hardly have been more dramatic. The lead see-sawed back and forth, and with each lead change a different group of St. Joe fans had bragging rights. The Yankees scored two runs in the top of the eighth to take a 7-4 lead, but the Pirates answered with five in the bottom of the inning to lead 9-7. In the top of the ninth, the Yankees tied the game 9-9 and everyone quieted down. The first Pirate batter in the bottom of the ninth was second baseman, Bill Mazeroski, who hit the ball over the left field fence to end the series. Pirate fans in the dorm went crazy in celebration of a World Series victory in which their team was outscored 55-27.

I was not much of a football fan, but Paul was a huge Cleveland Browns fan in the days when they had two legendary players, running back Jim Brown and place kicker Lou "The Toe" Groza. Vince Mixie, a funny and pretty strange guy Bill, Paul and I got to know well in our last two years, was from McKeesport just outside Pittsburgh. Vince, or "The Vinnie", was a jive-talking, weight-lifting, ex-military man.

The first time I met him, he joked, "I'm a diddy from the city. I smoke dope, jump rope, and watch Roy Rogers on my video scope." If you asked him "What's happening?" or as he preferred "What's shaking?," he'd say "Nothin' shakin' but the leaves on the trees, and they wouldn't be shakin' if it weren't for the breeze" or "Nothin' shakin' but the beans in the pot, and they wouldn't be shakin' if the water weren't hot."

The Vinnie was a rabid Pittsburgh Steelers fan. When the Browns played the Steelers on television, Vince always told Paul firmly "You *will* be on my right." It was an entertaining afternoon of barbs when the two of them watched the game together, and I learned to enjoy football a little as well.

* * *

In compliance with NCAA rules, I never received money for playing basketball at UD. For spending money, I saved as much as I could in the summers. Mom and Dad were not in a position to help me financially. In fact, Mom often said a book of stamps each month was her contribution to my college education. I'm not sure exactly what the NCAA rules were then, but there were a few perqs basketball players got regularly that may have been minor violations.

A local chain of pizza shops gave us coupons for free pizzas, and a downtown movie theater gave us free movie passes. We were given books of season tickets to Flyer home games, two books in our sophomore year, three in our junior year and four in our senior year. Supposedly these were for our family members and friends, but most of us sold them. Our travel uniform, a navy-blue blazer with gray slacks, was provided for us. I'm not sure if the Athletic Department or a local department store paid for them. As I mentioned earlier, my contact lenses were also provided free of charge.

I had enough money for incidentals and an occasional beer or soft drink and sandwich, but I didn't have much leeway. Dates tended to double my costs, so I passed up expensive events for students with dates. I was more aware than ever of how much material wealth some people had compared to me. Just looking at a person's clothes in their closet made that obvious.

Once after Christmas break, a friend confided he and his sister and brother had each been given $5,000 for Christmas as part of an inheritance. I recall getting some socks and underwear that year. Other students talked about the great family trips they

183

had taken or were going to take to Europe or other exotic destinations.

In my junior and senior years, a group of friends went to Fort Lauderdale over Spring Break and had a great time. This was when *Where the Boys Are* was a popular Connie Francis movie and song about college kids in Fort Lauderdale at Spring Break. Instead of going to Fort Lauderdale, I went to see the movie.

On weekday nights, Paul and I studied in the library after dinner until around 10:30, when Bill walked down to get us. I'm not sure what he did earlier in the evening, but we had voracious appetites and were ready for a snack. Our favorite was a big hamburger and RC Cola at a bar a couple of blocks from campus called Ray and Dot's. After that, I was usually ready for bed, but Paul studied longer if he had a test or big assignment coming up. There were parties and other social events all year long but we rarely participated until after the basketball season. On weekends if there was no game, we sometimes went to a movie.

Many UD students lived in apartments near campus. Some of them had the financial means and inclination to organize parties in their apartments for their friends on weekends. The party hosts provided beer, soft drinks and snack food. They usually played records of popular songs during the party; favorites were crooner Johnny Mathis's love songs. The hosts often asked people attending to contribute a little toward expenses.

Most of these parties were open to any UD student and were a popular form of inexpensive entertainment. Students who enjoyed the bar scene regularly went to a bar on Friday night and sometimes for a mid-week break on Wednesday night. Carl's Tavern just off Wyoming Street and Kramer's on Irving Avenue were two of the most popular bars.

Parties were mainly on weekends, and during my freshman year I went home when I could. As a sophomore, Bill had a car so we were able to get around town. Before that we used the city bus on evenings out. I attended a few parties in the spring, usually with Bill and Paul. We sometimes had dates, but often went alone as there were lots of unattached girls at most parties.

Bill had a girl back home then, but they were seeing other people and Paul and I had no ties. We occasionally stopped at Carl's or Kramer's to see who was there. We usually found some people who wanted to talk Flyer basketball. They bought our drinks and got us talking about next year or the previous one and what Blackburn intended to do about this or that.

In our junior year, Bill spied a beautiful freshman girl on campus and he was smitten. Her name was Jeanne Mack. Her friends knew Bill was interested in her but for some reason the two of them had not met before the NIT. On Saturday night after our big win in New York there were lots of parties in Flyer fans' rooms in the Picadilly and nearby hotels. I was with Bill and Paul at a party when someone invited me to another one nearby.

It happened Jeanne was there. I introduced myself and told her I was a friend of Bill's. She was interested when I mentioned he was at a nearby party and was anxious to meet her. A little shy at first, but she eventually agreed to go with me to meet Bill. They hit it off immediately. Soon after that Paul met a sorority sister and good friend of Jeanne's, Ruth Bohne, and they began a steady relationship.

With my two best friends at UD practically engaged, I was often the odd man out in our senior year. I dated three or four different girls that year and sometimes Ruth or Jeanne fixed me up with one of their friends, but I wasn't interested in anything serious. Ruth and Jeanne kidded me over the years about all the trouble they had finding me dates. After basketball was over and graduation was approaching, I wondered if I may regret not meeting a future wife among all these college girls. I continued to date a UD girl over the summer, but it didn't work out in the end.

In the summers, I lived with Ed and socialized more with him than with my college friends. Our house was on Meridian Street on the east side, a few blocks from Chuck Frey's Tavern just off East Fifth Street. Chuck had some past connection with Mercer County, and Ed and I got to be pretty good friends with him. He had a helper in the bar named Shorty, who Ed always called Shortly.

Sometimes we met Bill, Paul, and Dan, who lived in Dayton during those summers, at Chuck's place for a few beers. Bill lived in an apartment near UD and was recreation director at Wonderly Park in Oakwood. My teammates and I went to the park in the late afternoon one or two days a week to play pickup basketball, mostly with other college players home for the summer. I also played on a slow-pitch softball team with Ed and Dick Kemper one or two nights a week.

I rode home with Ed and Dick after work each Friday in the summers. At home, I played slow-pitch softball for Sharpsburg's team on Sunday afternoon, and usually went to a dance with my high school social group, including Oscar, Harry and Jerry. Sometimes we took girls home from the dance, or I double dated with Oscar or one of my other friends. I enjoyed watching Jim's baseball games on Saturday afternoons or evenings. He pitched for an American Legion team from Coldwater for a couple of summers near the end of high school and later for Fort Recovery's Legion team for five years.

* * *

As for my senior year in basketball, I considered a chapter title mirroring the previous chapter, namely, "A Season to Forget", but that was too negative. Big disappointments were balanced by nice memories. At the time of our NIT victory, the prospects for 1962-63 were bright but for the second year in a row the Flyers had some shocking surprises. The first came in spring of 1962 in the form of probation by the NCAA barring us from post-season tournaments for the next two years. The specific charges were too many freshmen games in 1960-61 and the financing of three trips for Roger to testify in New York.

We knew from the beginning we would not go to a postseason tournament in 1962-63. Disappointing, but I was surprised how much the absence of that goal meant toward the end of a long 26-game season. Without it, the only motivations for the players, coach, and fans are personal pride, competitive spirit, and desire to have as good a won-loss record as possible. We weren't in a conference so the won-loss record was only important to us; no competitors were trying to best it. We gave our best effort, but it was hard to obtain a high level of intensity like we had in the NIT.

In late September and early October of 1962 when the national collegiate basketball magazines appeared, UD was highlighted favorably in spite of our probation. Chim got lots of attention and was named first-team All-American center, Gordie and I were mentioned and pictured, too, and the team was predicted to be in the top five or ten in the country.

Official practice began on October 15 as usual. One afternoon in late October, I was walking down the hill to the Fieldhouse for practice when Chim came up the hill toward me. It was a bolt out of the blue for me when he said, "I'm packing and going home. Hold them together this year, Harry." I asked him what in the world happened, and he said he couldn't afford to stay without financial help. He had gotten married over the summer, and his wife was expecting a baby. I wished him well and didn't see him again for 40 years.

On top of our probation, Chim's leaving was difficult for the team to take, but life and basketball go on. On a Friday in November a week or two before our first game, Tom told the team I would be captain. He announced it to the public on his television show the next Sunday afternoon. "Schoen is an exemplary young man, a good student who leads by example," was the way he put it on his show. I was pleased to be captain and appreciated his comments.

Other positive news, Tom recruited 6'11" Hank Finkel who had played for one year at St. Peter's College in New Jersey. He was redshirted in 1962-63, but he practiced with us all year. Strong with wide shoulders, Hank had a nice touch on his left-handed hook and push shots within ten or so feet of the basket. He couldn't jump well but he was very hard to defend and rebound against. He had a great career at UD where he was the third leading career scorer, then played eight years in the NBA. Hank was also a nice guy who was popular with his teammates.

Gordie and me on the cover of the program of our first '62-'63 game.

We were not a bad team, finishing 16-10 with nine of our ten losses on the road. We swept two each from Xavier, Miami and Duquesne and split with Louisville and DePaul. We narrowly lost away games to the ultimate 1963 NCAA champion, Loyola of Chicago, and NCAA runner-up, UC, by five and seven points, respectively. Bill Westerkamp, who had started as a sophomore, took over the center spot again as a senior. Sophomore Bob Sullivan played opposite me at forward, and my roommate Dan Mueller teamed with Gordie at guard in most games.

Junior Chuck Izor was usually sixth man coming in at guard or forward. If Bill needed a break, I played center or senior Ron Anello came in. Paul and juniors Jimmy Powers and Don Smith also saw some playing time at guard. Our scoring was pretty well balanced with Gordie around 15 points per game, Bill, Dan, and I in the 11 to 13 range, and Sully around eight or nine. My high game totals were 21 against Central State and 19 against Toledo.

In our game at Louisville, I was caught in a pressure packed situation. We were down by two points when I grabbed an offensive rebound and was fouled just as time ran out. Coach Hickman called timeout so I had time to get nervous. On our bench, there was nothing to talk about or prepare for. We lost the game if I missed either free throw. I remember thinking if I remained calm and kept my shot in its natural rhythm, chances were good I'd hit it. Then I stepped to the line, the only player on the court in gigantic Freedom Hall in front of over 8,000 hostile UL fans. When the referee handed me the ball, the fans yelled, screamed, stomped on the floor, and waved their arms wildly – anything they could do to distract me.

As always on free throws, I bounced the ball three times, took a deep breath and let it out slowly feeling my muscles relax. Strangely, the basket appeared smaller and further away than usual. I tried to ignore that illusion and shoot with exactly the motion and push I had used a million times. The first shot swished, nothing but net.

Again, Hickman called a timeout so I could think some more, but I stayed calm and kept in rhythm with the same result. The game went into overtime, but my heroics were for naught as we lost anyway. Tom said something in the newspapers about that being one of the gutsiest feats he had seen as a coach.

The season had its lighter moments as fans and a sportswriter had some fun with my name. A popular song in 1962 was *Danke Schoen* sung by Wayne Newton. At home games, the fans on our end of the court had a good time yelling or singing "dunk it Schoen" during our layup drills in pregame warm ups. One of the Dayton sportswriters wrote a column in which he connected my name to the title of an older song, *Bei Mir Bist du Schoen*. Ed loved that sort of thing and over the years he sometimes referred to me as "Bistra Schoen."

Early in the season, an article appeared on the sports pages about Jerry Lucas, who was an intelligent guy and a great rebounder, saying he was able to tell where a rebound would go

189

using physics. Tom knew I was a good student, and more than once accused me of being too smart for my own good in basketball. He asked me how Lucas could do that. Maybe there was some physics he should be teaching his players.

I mentioned the angle of incidence and angle of reflection equality, but that was obvious to an athlete from experience and not worth teaching in a formal way. After Tom and I talked it over a little, we decided Lucas was a great rebounder more because of his athletic abilities and experience than his knowledge of physics.

I remembered lots of batting averages from the 1955 major league season having played that season's edition of APBA baseball six or eight years earlier. When anything came up about that season, I quoted a batting average or two, sometimes of some obscure players. Paul thought I was just kidding around and making the averages up. I assured him they were right on target, but we went back and forth about that for a while.

Finally, we agreed to a bet. Paul could choose any fifty players from the 1955 *Who's Who in Baseball*, and I bet I knew the batting average of at least 40 of them within ten points above or below their exact average. We followed up on the bet on a team bus trip to play nearby rival, Miami of Ohio. I got 44 of 50 averages and won the bet. Blackburn heard the ruckus and asked what was going on. He just shook his head when we explained it to him.

In Chicago to play Loyola on New Year's Eve, a group of us went to see *Taras Bulba*, a movie starring Yul Brynner. In the movie, Taras Bulba was a Cossack leader in the Middle Ages. When Tom heard about it, he made fun of me for taking the guys to see Tulip Bulbs. He mentioned Tulip Bulbs several times on that trip, laughing every time. I was reminded of how much fun he had when I was a freshman kidding us about losing to the Little Sisters of the Poor.

Unfortunately, the season ended on a sour note at DePaul. We lost by two points in the last seconds of the game. I don't remember exactly what happened, but Tom blamed Gordie and me. In the locker room after the game, he chewed us both out, which for me was the final time. I was used to his coaching methods by then, but it was still exasperating to have our player-coach relationship end in that way.

The season was marred by a tragedy on the night of January 16 1963, when Tom Luppe, a UD frosh forward from Pittsburgh, collapsed on the floor and died of cardiac arrest. As a senior, I was treasurer of the Varsity D Club, which decided to sponsor the Thomas M. Luppe Memorial Award starting in 1964 and continuing annually to the present. The annual recipient is a freshman player who displays the courage, desire, and moral integrity characteristic of Tom Luppe. The president of the club was a football player, so he assigned me the task of announcing the award at the annual UD basketball banquet a few weeks after the end of the season.

The main award at the banquet, the team's most valuable player, went to Gordie. I had the highest free throw percentage at 79% and was the senior with the highest grade point average. Paul and I were both a little over 3.3 but my gpa was a few hundredths of a point higher. I received the scholastic award, but it would have made more sense for Paul and me to share it. The free throw award was called the Alex Schoen Award after a captain of the basketball team in the 1920s or 1930s. One reporter wrote Hal (no relation) Schoen won the Alex Schoen Award. Ed picked up on the "no relation" and used it in our future correspondence

Having the floor near the end of the banquet to announce the Luppe Award, I took the opportunity to thank Coach Blackburn, saying "He didn't make men out of all of us, but he tried awfully hard." Then I said, more or less, "On behalf of the seniors, it will be a long time before we forget the 1962 NIT, but our association with the wonderful Dayton fans is something we will never forget."

My remarks at the banquet impressed someone, as I got a letter in a few days from a man in the personnel department at Goodyear Rubber in Akron Ohio. I'm not sure if the writer had been at the banquet or someone who had been there recommended me, but the letter urged me to apply for a public relations job with the company and play on the Goodyear semipro National Industrial Basketball Association team. This was basketball at a high level and some players used it as a path to the NBA. After giving the letter serious thought, I decided not to pursue it. I wanted to get started on my career as a mathematics teacher and coach.

* * *

The Flyers were not allowed to play as a college team in the NIT or NCAA tournaments, but after the season seniors were free to play wherever and whenever we had the opportunity. For charity or just to make a buck, sports promoters organized spring tournaments that drew on the pool of college senior players. One such tournament was in Wheelersburg, Ohio, on the Ohio River.

A friend of mine who knew the tournament organizers recruited me to play on one of the teams. Most of my teammates were small college players, who I didn't know and had never practiced with. I assumed I was one of the top players on the team, so I played center and wasn't shy about shooting. The opposing center was no match for me. I scored 43 points on drives, hook shots, turn-around jumpers, and offensive rebounds. After the game, the local organizers declared they had never seen anyone play the middle as well as I did.

That game was on a Saturday in late March or early April. The next Monday I stopped at Blackburn's office for some reason. He said, "I hear you got 43 points in Wheelersburg this weekend." I don't know how he had heard, but I mumbled, "the competition wasn't very good."

"That's a lot of points against any competition," he replied, to my surprise. That comment was as close as I ever got to a face-to-face compliment from Tom Blackburn.

I played in another tournament a few weeks later with much better competition. It was the Sportsman-YMCA tournament in Charleston, West Virginia. The teams were made up of college seniors and current NBA players. Jerry West, a great guard at West Virginia University in the late fifties and at that time an all-star NBA player for the Los Angeles Lakers, was the local hero. He played in the tournament in the two previous years and was not on the winning team, so to increase the chances of a victory for West's team the tournament organizers put Celtic great Bill Russell and another former WVU all-American and current NBA player, Rod (Hot Rod) Hundley, on his team. Our team was four UD seniors, a Flyer of the class of 1961 (Pat Allen), a couple of small college players and one substitute NBA center named Bud Olsen who was from Dayton.

We played West and Russell's team in the first game. I guarded West, who was much too quick for me but we didn't have anyone else who could challenge him. I didn't challenge him much either, as he scored 36 points, six or eight more than his season per game average, mostly on long jumpers he got off too quickly for me to react. I scored 20, hitting jump shots from outside and sometimes driving underneath.

Bill Russell is considered one of the best defensive men in NBA history, so I have to tell my grandchildren about a drive underneath that still stands out in my memory. As I drove toward the basket I knew Russell was close behind and would try to block my shot, so I made a head fake as if to go up on the right side and continued on under the basket for a left-handed reverse layup. An instant after I released the ball Russell's hand brushed against my palm, just missing a block, as the ball went into the basket. I had driven against the great Bill Russell and scored.

In the consolation game, I scored 14 points playing head to head against 6'8" NBA forward Len Chappel, a former star at Wake Forest. He scored just eight points but we lost, finishing fourth of four teams in the tournament.

* * *

As I began to mull over what to do after graduation, Ed suggested I take advantage of my celebrity status by opening a bar in Dayton called "Captain Hal Schoen's NIT Bar." More practical advice came from the chairman of the Mathematics Department, Dr. Kenneth Schraut, who invited me to apply to the UD's Master of Science program in mathematics. The idea interested me and I filed it away as "maybe someday," but my academic major prepared me to be a high school mathematics teacher and coach. I wanted to give that profession a try. Doc Schraut understood and said to let him know if I changed my mind in a few years.

Having decided on the nature of my work, the next goal was to find a job. Soon after basketball season ended, I heard Archbishop Alter High School, a new Catholic school in the Dayton suburb of Kettering, was hiring a basketball coach and the principal hoped I'd apply. I was undecided about staying in the Dayton area, but I submitted my application and waited.

The principal called and scheduled an interview for me at the school at 4:00 one afternoon in late March or early April. I borrowed Bill's car. I thought I knew how to get to Alter High School, but when I came to the street I turned right instead of left. After driving a mile or two, I noted my mistake and hurried to the school arriving about 15 minutes late.

I apologized and explained what happened, but the principal was angry about my tardiness even giving me a brief lecture. When he calmed down, I had a job interview but it was pretty awkward for me. The principal talked about the school and the athletic program, but he didn't ask much about me or give me any indication he was interested in hiring me. I wrote the job off and decided I'd better keep looking.

One afternoon a week or so later, an athletic department secretary called and told me to come to the Fieldhouse as soon as I could. Father Robert Kitchin, a principal from a new Catholic high school in Indianapolis was there. He had driven to UD with the hope of recruiting a basketball coach for Bishop Chartrand High School on the south side of Indianapolis.

Mike McMahon (40) for XU was also hired by Chartrand High School. We became friends, and Mike was in my wedding party.

We talked for quite a while. He was a great salesman for the school, and he had examined my student records and loved that I taught math. According to him, I was exactly what they needed. The salary, $5,100, was modest but about 300 or 400 dollars more than at Alter. I took his phone number and said I'd talk to my parents, think it over and get back to him in a few days.

I accepted the job. Sometime later I heard from a third party that the Alter principal was disappointed and thought I should have called him before accepting another job. It was too late. I was looking forward to the next phase of my life, teaching math and coaching basketball and baseball at Chartrand High School in Indianapolis.

AFTERWARD

In my first year of teaching and coaching, I met Theresa Maloney on a blind date two days after the assassination of President John Kennedy. I was finally ready for a serious relationship and fortunately Theresa was, too. We were married on June 6, 1964, and at this writing are in our fifty-fourth year of marriage. Tragically, we lost our first baby, a premature son, Joseph, at five and a half months, but then had two beautiful, bright, healthy daughters, Mary in 1966 and Jenny in 1968.

I had an interesting and generally successful four years of high school teaching and coaching with some pleasant sports memories. During that time I attended Indiana University at night and in the summers and earned my MS in Mathematics Education, and I was ready for a change. I decided to pursue further graduate education with the goal of becoming a college professor. I took Doc Schraut up on his earlier offer and returned to UD as a math instructor and student in the MS in Mathematics

Mom and Dad see their two oldest sons awarded the MS in Mathematics by UD

program. By then, Jim had worked his way to his BS in Mathematics in 1967 while pitching for the UD baseball team. We were in the master's program together for two years and both received our MS degrees in May 1969.

That fall I entered the PhD in Mathematics Education program at Ohio State University, earning my degree in 1971. I then began a 34-year career as a jointly appointed Professor of Mathematics and Education. The first three years were at Virginia Tech in Blacksburg and the final 31 at the University of Iowa in Iowa City. Some people complain about the "publish or perish" requirements for faculty at large universities, but I always enjoyed research and writing as well as teaching. My scholarly work focused on high school mathematics teaching and curriculum. I also served from 1990 to 1993 as Chairman of the UI Division of Curriculum & Instruction.

Meanwhile, Theresa was committed to staying home with our pre-school daughters, but when she could she conscientiously pursued her own career in professional education. When we were married she had one and a half years toward a bachelor's

Hal & Theresa Schoen family; early 1970s

degree in elementary education, and she taught at Saint Mark's Catholic school in Indianapolis until Mary was born. In Dayton, Blacksburg and Iowa City, she continued to work on her degree part time while she was a stay-at-home Mom. Upon finishing her bachelor's degree at UI in 1975 and with both daughters in school, she resumed her career, the first year as a half-time teacher in the Iowa City Public Schools.

The next year she was half time in the classroom and a half-time assistant principal. The administrative part of her job required she begin part-time work on a Master's degree in Education, and she obtained the degree in three years while continuing at her job. When the principal position opened at Penn Elementary in the Iowa City District, Theresa was hired serving there for ten years. During this time, she continued in graduate school earning her PhD in Curriculum & Instruction at UI. A couple of years later she joined the faculty at Coe College, a small Liberal Arts school in Cedar Rapids, as a Professor in the Teacher Education Department for six years before dropping back to part time in 1999.

Theresa receives a 1988 National Distinguished Principal Award from U.S. Secretary of Education, Henry Cisnaros, as two officers of the National Association of Elementary School Principals look on.

Jenny and Mary were both married in Iowa City in 1993, Jenny to Dale Strabala and Mary to Joe Merchant. Both are fine men who we feel blessed to have in our family. Each couple has three children. In the Merchant family, Chris (21) is a junior at Grinnell College in Iowa, Amelia (19) is a first-year student at Colorado College, and Catherine (14) is in eighth grade in Ames,

Iowa. As for the Strabalas, Grace (14) is in ninth grade, Jack (12) is in sixth grade, and Rose (7) is in first grade all in Indianapolis. Theresa and I are extremely proud of our family.

Thanksgiving 2014: First row, l to r: Catherine, Theresa, Rose, me, Grace. Back row: Amelia, Chris, Joe, Mary, Jenny, Dale, Jack

By most measures my siblings have been successful in both their family lives and their work careers. Jim earned his PhD in Mathematics from the University of Cincinnati in 1974 and spent most of his professional career at NCR in Dayton. On the sports side, Jim and I are the only brothers to both score over 1,000 points in our basketball careers at FRHS and both be inducted into the FRHS Athletic Hall of Fame. Rick earned a PhD in Mathematics from Stanford in 1977 where he also spent many years as a distinguished professor and researcher in Differential Geometry. He has won several prestigious awards for his work including a 1983 MacArthur Foundation Fellowship (the so-called "genius" award) and a 2017 Wolf Prize in Mathematics.

My sisters Janice, Doris, and Marilyn earned nursing degrees

200

Rick and wife Doris Fischer-Colbrie in Sweden for conferring of Rick's honorary DSc degree from the University of Warwick

Dan at the National Spelling Contest in Washington, DC.

and had successful careers in healthcare. Pat has done exceptional historical research and writing about the Fort Recovery area and about our family. Dan, who as a fifth grader in 1965 won the southwest Ohio regional spelling contest for grades five through eight, had a productive career as a businessman in Fort Recovery. Dan's spelling contest victory was a great family moment as the rest of us were at Pat and Neil's wedding reception watching him on a Dayton television station.

All my siblings who have children raised them with love and support. The next generation of the family, that is, my daughters, nieces, and nephews, are well established in the educated middle class of America. Our family's story is the story of upward social mobility, the American Dream.

Since I was the first to attend UD, the family has developed a deep connection there. Three of my brothers, a sister-in-law, a brother-in-law, and seven nieces and nephews have attended since, not to mention spouses of nieces and nephews. Rick was named a UD Distinguished Alumnus and won the UD Special

Neil, Pat, Jim, Mary Ann, Theresa, me in California for Rick's son's wedding

Achievement Award. I am listed as a Distinguished Scholar Athlete Alumnus. In 2007, some of my siblings and I established the Arnold P. and Rose M. Schoen Scholarship Fund at UD to help support an able but financially needy undergraduate mathematics major.

As for UD basketball, Tom Blackburn died of lung cancer in spring of 1964, the year after I graduated, so I never knew him as anything but my coach. Don Donoher was named head coach beginning the next year. Don had many good seasons. His strong teams in the late 1960s combined with Blackburn's gave the Flyers the most wins of any major college basketball team in the combined decades of the 1950s and 1960s, edging out UCLA and Kentucky. This record included 256 wins versus just 33 losses in the UD Fieldhouse from 1950 until the present UD Arena opened in 1969-70. Don was inducted into the National Basketball Hall of Fame in 2015 in recognition of his distinguished career as Flyer coach.

Roger Brown worked in a factory in Dayton after he was

banned from UD and the NBA. He played AAU basketball in Dayton until 1967, when at age 26 he was the first player signed by the Indiana Pacers in the new American Basketball Association. Oscar Robertson had recommended him to the Pacers management. In the early 1970s, Roger was awarded a large financial settlement from the NBA as restitution for his wrongful disbarment in 1961. In spite of missing six of his prime basketball years, Roger had an outstanding ABA career and was named to the Naismith Memorial Basketball Hall of Fame in 2014.

FRHS friends: First row, l to r: Marilyn (Brunswick) Bubp, Theresa, Alma Kemper. Second row: Tom Bubp, Oscar Jutte, me, Ed. Suzie Jutte took the picture.

My best friends from my youth, Ed Kemper, Oscar Jutte, Bill Westerkamp and Paul Winterhalter, were all successful in their professions as were my cousins, Harry and Jerry, who took over their father's farm and worked in local factories. Bob Fiely coached at FRHS for five years, my senior year and Jim's four years. He re-entered the military in 1963 where he stayed until retirement. The entire group has experienced the joys and challenges of long, stable marriages with children and grandchildren.

Reunion at UD Arena, l to r: Ruth, Paul, Bill, me, Jeanne. Theresa took the picture

My brothers and sisters and I had some fruitful discussions as I worked on the first four chapters about my childhood memories We came to appreciate how unique our individual childhood experiences were, though we had the same parents and grew up in the same family. For example, many of my brothers and sisters were surprised reading Chapter 2 on farm work that Dad seemed so important to me. I was also surprised how many of my vivid memories included Dad and often in a positive way.

My younger siblings commented on how different their own memories were from mine. They remembered Mom and Dad at more advanced ages and were too young to remember the evolution of farm work I wrote so much about. Some of my sisters expressed surprise that I had so many chores, as they didn't remember the boys working much compared to them.

Mom's 99th birthday: my siblings and in-laws are pictured except for Doris & Doug, Rick & Doris, and Janice's husband Harold.

Certainly my sisters had lots of responsibilities that for the older ones included motherly duties Mom was stretched too thin to handle herself. My youngest sister Marilyn remembers Kate as being like a mother to her.

After many years as a college professor, my roots continue to be an important part of my identity. When I retired from the University of Iowa in 2005, my former doctoral students organized a small retirement party attended by about twenty-five ex-students, a few faculty member friends, and spouses. At the end of an evening of roasting and thanking me, I was prepared to make brief remarks reminiscing about life at the University of Iowa that the audience would appreciate.

By the time I spoke, I was caught up in the sentiments of the moment. I deviated from my prepared remarks and spoke from my heart, "I am from a humble background growing up on a small family farm in western Ohio with twelve brothers and sisters. My parents didn't graduate from high school. I've always felt very fortunate and proud to be a professor at the University of Iowa."

Snowbirds

ACKNOWLEDGMENTS

First and foremost, thanks to Theresa Maloney Schoen for her love and support during the last 54 plus years. On this project, she read drafts carefully and made many helpful suggestions. As always, she is my biggest supporter in many ways, including spreading the word about my memoirs and keeping my spirits up when I feel discouraged.

Thanks to all my siblings who read drafts and suggested improvements. In particular, Kate, Janice, and Rick provided details about their role in several of the stories. Special thanks to Pat for her help in pulling together family photos, for allowing me open access to the information she has accumulated about the family, and for her suggestions for improvement of the manuscript. My deepest appreciation to Jim for his insightful comments on drafts, for providing many pictures, and for doing a final reading of the entire manuscript.

My thanks also to Cyndie Gerken for her generous advice and encouragement based on her experience as an author with CreateSpace. And finally, thanks to the CreateSpace staff for their professional help in the printing process and the beautiful cover design.

All of you have collaborated in making this a better book than it would otherwise have been.

ABOUT THE AUTHOR

Harold L. (Hal) Schoen was a high school mathematics teacher and baseball and basketball coach for four years after earning his BS degree in 1963. Upon completing the necessary graduate education, he spent 34 years as a jointly appointed Professor of Mathematics and Education. He is author of high school and beginning college mathematics textbooks and has written many professional papers. *Growing Up* is his first attempt at writing for a more general audience.

An avid reader and movie fan, he particularly enjoys history, historical novels, and movies based on them. Until his early forties, he played recreation league basketball and slow-pitch softball. Since retiring from sports competition, he enjoys recreational biking, hiking and swimming. His favorite college basketball teams are the Dayton Flyers, Iowa Hawkeyes, and Butler Bulldogs. He is no longer the enthusiastic fan of major league baseball that he was in his youth, but he enjoys a few evenings each summer with his family watching the AAA Indianapolis Indians play at Victory Field.

A University of Iowa Professor Emeritus since he retired in 2005, he is a dedicated husband, father and grandfather. Since 1999, he and his wife Theresa have spent two or three of the coldest winter months in a condominium on the west coast of Florida. Taking advantage of the warm weather, the two of them love walking and resting on the beach. They also enjoy hosting family and friends on visits to Florida.

Hal's author website is www.amazon.com/author/halschoen

208

Made in the USA
Lexington, KY
16 November 2017